Does This Volvo Make My Butt Look Big?

Thoughts for moms
and other tired people

Annabel Monaghan

Fischer Press Books • New York

ISBN-13: 9780692826508
ISBN-10: 0692826505
Library of Congress Control Number:2016921410
Fischer Press, Rye, New York

For Tom

(You might want to stop reading here.)

Foreword

Marriage, friendship and parenting — each of us comes at them from a different angle. Mothering can be an isolating, chaotic, competitive sport, with plenty of moments when we fall far short of perfect. Throw in a leaky boiler and a couple of surly teenagers, and most of us don't have a clue what comes next. Social media dictates that we're supposed to be living thrilling lives, enjoying fabulous relationships and fulfilling careers. We home bake and hand make. Our children never fall off the school honor roll, and boy, do we have the bumper stickers to prove it! So nothing is more welcome, more refreshing, than when someone lets down her hair and gets real.

This collection of essays by Annabel Monaghan is that kick in the pants that we all need to remind us we're in it together, and none of us have it all figured out. Each chapter is so finely crafted, so perfectly turned and taut, that I marvel at the construct of the finished product. As a writer, they make me want to rip out the seams and study how she assembles them.

Annabel's gift is to perfectly capture life's behind-the-scenes moments, the quiet, humorous thoughts and observations we make every day. She gives us permission to laugh at ourselves, and her essays invite us to join her as she turns her lighter lens on the wash, rinse, spin, repeat cycle of our ordinary days.

It's not easy to get a giggle out of someone with just the printed word. And it's also far more difficult than it seems to write about the everyday, universal truths of motherhood without sounding preachy, whiny or like an Aesop's Fable. The key is her distinctive voice. Annabel is wry and humorous, truthful and self-deprecating. Her writing combines the brilliance of Nora Ephron's wit and Erma Bombeck's madcap housewifery, with a dash of Liz Gilbert's heartfelt girlfriend truth.

How did she grab that cartoon thought bubble over my head? I think. *When did she sneak a camera into my bedroom? How did she capture my life so perfectly?*

These essays are freeze-frame moments, as delightful as discovering a sand dollar on a beach or finding a blue jay feather in the grass. The Ziploc bag goldfish from the school fair, the chronic recurrence of dinner, the awkward parent-teacher conference. They are simple, beautiful and funny. And did I already mention that Annabel is very, very funny? But she can also be incredibly poignant, tackling heavier emotional subjects, like sending kids off to college, or the ups and downs of a long-term marriage.

Every so often a piece of writing reaches down into your chest cavity and plucks out your beating heart. That's what happened when I first read her essay "Growing up in a Marriage." I blinked back tears. I read and reread it, and clipped it out of our newspaper to save in my "special file." When you read this essay, I dare you not to be awed by the range of emotions she evokes in just a few short pages. But then there are so many of those stories in here.

Full disclosure, Annabel Monaghan lives in my town. Yup, I get to bump into her at the grocery store and on the sidewalk of our main street as we run our mom errands. And I was honored when she asked if I would write the foreword to this book. Because I know her, I feel compelled to tell you that in real life she is just as self-deprecating, cute as a button and hysterically funny as she is on these pages. (Gosh darn it all!)

She's the person you'd call if your dad broke his hip, and you needed a ride to the airport. She'd have the best orthodontist recommendation or know the recipe for kohlrabi salad. Heck, she would even know what kohlrabi was! And she'd be the one organizing a girlfriend getaway, with lots of red wine. She's just that girl. We all want to be her friend.

And when you finish this book, when you've read and read aloud and shared these essays, when you've smiled and nodded and grabbed the tissues, you too will be her friend. And you will marvel, as I did, at how easy and effortless she makes it all look, and how much better you feel for having spent a little time with her voice in your head.

Lee Woodruff

August 2016

My Paper Piles — Why I Still Haven't
Registered My Kids for Camp

I've never really been one for spring cleaning. Spring seems like such an arbitrary time to organize your life, clean your closets and generally get your house together. I mean we've usually just come off of three months of shut-in weather, so if I haven't done it by March 21, it's just not going to happen. But I always hold out hope that it might happen next year, because Future Me loves this sort of thing. She tackles paperwork with pure joy, she scrapbooks, she RSVPs on time. She carries tissues in her purse. She is detail oriented and dangerously fit. I just adore her, but today all I have is Present Me.

Present Me doesn't really mind the great mass of paper strewn around my kitchen. I suspect my Present Husband does, so I try. My version of spring cleaning is straightening the piles and then remarking to myself what nice straight edges I've made. Report cards, bills, coupons, insurance forms and medical clearance packets that were due weeks and weeks ago have become part of my visual landscape.

But even tidied, those piles aren't going anywhere. They have a healthy pulse and a voracious appetite for reproduction. Every day, the mail makes its way inside, and the backpacks seem to spew sign-up sheets, reminders and sticky self-portraits. The paper multiplies like so many wet Gremlins. Or the laundry. I eyeball one pile that is about eight inches high. *How many paper-thin liabilities does it take to make a pile that high,* I wonder. Future Me is proactive and full of enthusiasm for finding out. Present Me kinda wants a nap.

I know I'll have to actually tackle them all before tax time, but the problem is that each piece of paper sets into motion a complicated chain of to-dos that seems like it's better suited for tomorrow than today. A simple camp registration form, for example, necessitates a call to the pediatrician to schedule checkups. I look up the number, sit on hold, negotiate a post-3 p.m. time for all three of my children to come in — provided it's after basketball season, before baseball season and not on a Wednesday because of religion class. I have to be extra friendly on the phone to convince the scheduler that I am not insane. I hang up with a pit in my stomach, because I know she knows.

That task, completed in nine minutes and at great personal expense, is just the first step in getting that one piece of paper out of the pile. To the naked eye, that pile will still be eight inches high when I'm done. I try a different approach: I sort. I take the pile and make it into three less intimidating piles. The first pile is stuff that has to be dealt with or my water will be turned off and my kids will be home all summer. I label it "Code Red" and straighten it furiously. The next pile is stuff that means something to my husband but not to me. I mark it "Tom" and put it out of my line of vision. I'm really getting somewhere.

The next pile (rejoice!) is stuff that I should have dealt with, but now it's too late so I can throw it out. It's the order form for the yearbooks, a flyer for a seminar I wanted to attend back in the fall, a request for me to make cookies for a bake sale that was yesterday, and a note home saying someone in my kid's class had lice. As these things seem to have worked themselves out with no involvement on my part, I sashay to the recycling bin and rid myself of three inches of paper, secretly happy that I forgot about the yearbook. It's just more paper, bound in cardboard.

Now I'm left with just a two-inch pile that's not my problem and my three-inch Code Red pile. I go back to the camp registration forms and see that they want me to provide my kids' T-shirt sizes. That really just involves looking at the ones from last year and going up a size, but they're all the way in the attic. So I pick up the next paper. This one's not so bad — the insurance company wants me to call to verify my date of birth. I hold it determinedly in my hand while I make tea. And then I put it down without calling because I have a great idea ...

I decide to make a subcategory called "Problems That Can Be Solved With a Checkbook." I pay three bills and see that my pile is down to two inches. It's two inches of Code Red, but still, I've made some progress. Future Me is going to be so proud. And she can take it from here.

The Game of Life

The great thing about Candy Land and Chutes and Ladders is that they can be played in less than 15 minutes, and they take very little mental effort. Even so, when my husband comes home from work, I can still add "played a board game with the kids" to my list of heroic accomplishments. I could be on the phone (or even writing this book) and breeze through one of those games, no problem. Unfortunately, my five-year-old has developed an unhealthy interest in The Game of Life, the only game I know that is possibly more complicated than life itself.

At first I try to convince him that the little cars that lead us down life's path are there to be zoomed, and that whoever gets to the end first wins. But he isn't having it. So I figure if we are going to have to play, we'll do it right. I'll teach him a few Life lessons and get the dialogue going about the world around us. You know, actual parenting. Like on TV. We are just finishing up the ten minutes it takes to set up the game when I remember that he doesn't know how to read. This could be painful.

The game starts with each player at age 18, and I am pleased to see that he chooses to go to college. Having made such a wise choice, he faces a lot of career options after graduation. I encourage him to choose the accounting job because it comes with the possibility of the highest salary card. To my horror, he chooses to be a singer because, he claims, that's what he likes to do. "Why would I do something I don't like just for the money?" he asks. *Sigh.* He's got a lot to learn.

Meandering through Life, we each stop to get married. He thinks carefully before choosing a pink peg for his spouse rather than a blue one. He buys a house, which he also chooses for its color. Later I have to inform him that someone robbed his house and that he should have bought the insurance like I told him to. "I didn't know I'd get robbed." Ah, an actual Life lesson!

He rejoices every time he lands on a square that gives him another baby. He fills up his car with the allotted four children and then hoards the extras, laying them at the feet of his other kids in the back seat. (I have another son who likes to collect the child pegs too, but he leaves them on the side of the board with his money, claiming, "I don't want those kids riding in my car." We refer to him as The Smart One.)

Life gets more complicated as you move along. He wants to know what a Pulitzer Prize is and if it comes with candy. He wants to know who has the Solution to Pollution and why anyone would want to swim across the English Channel. I can only answer one of those. At some point I find myself explaining what a stock is, then what a dividend is and what taxes are for. And how dividends are taxed at a lower rate than ordinary income and why Warren Buffet doesn't really like that.

As Life winds down, we are laden with cash and real estate and lucky heirs, and we race toward retirement. If you can afford it, you get to retire in Millionaire Estates, and if you can't, Life relegates you to Countryside Acres. Before you enter either, you sell your house, the price of which is determined by a random spin of the wheel. That actually sounds about right.

Life ends, and I realize I've just spent a full hour explaining to a five-year-old how life works. I wait for the applause and maybe a little confetti as we each count up our money to determine who wins. And because I chose the rejected accounting job with the coveted yellow salary card, I have the most money. I tell him with great humility that I have won, and he has lost. He shakes his head and shows me his full little car, "I have the most family. I win."

I may need to rethink a few things.

Survivor: The Birthday Party

For my oldest son's fourth birthday, I took 15 kids on safari in my apartment building's backyard. I transformed the space into the African savanna and led them all in pith helmets and sunglasses on the adventure of a lifetime. I was living in New York City at the time and took three separate trips downtown to a professional theater supply shop for equipment. There were lifelike animals, games led by me, a cake shaped like a lion and elaborate safari themed party favors. I spent more time and mental energy planning that party than I did on my wedding.

My son remembers nothing about that day. But the photographs are great —so great that I'm hoping I can convince him he's actually been to Africa. More than a decade later, I've hosted a lot more birthday parties with varying degrees of difficulty. And I've learned a thing or two about the word "necessary." My youngest son turned eight today, and I am writing this with 110 minutes to spare before his party starts. I'm not saying I've conquered the birthday party, but I am happy to report that I am currently devoid of a migraine, a facial tic or a dangerously high blood alcohol level. Please benefit from my experience:

1. Manage your expectations. The party is only going to be fun if you're a child. Don't plan to enjoy your child's birthday party, or even your child at that birthday party. That twinkle in his eye isn't joy, it's madness. Children understand scarcity, that this only happens once a year for two hours. They're going to party like they mean it, and it might get ugly.

The stress of having to keep track of 15 kids at once makes you wonder about any social construct that supports the drop-off birthday party.

These are not soldiers we're managing, they are little children hopped up on sugar. Throw in variables like vomiting, the weather and the clown not showing up and, really, anything can happen.

One year for a fifth birthday, I had 20 kids over for a backyard extravaganza, and naturally, it poured rain. So I ended up with 20 kids playing tag in my house. Carrying chocolate cake. I found one little girl hiding with her cake in my bedroom. Quick on the uptake, she saw me and wiped her hands clean on my drapes and then stashed the rest of the cake in my husband's sock drawer. I appreciated her discretion. Which really brings me to what probably should have been my first point...

2. Don't have the party at home. It's funny that we throw these parties on the anniversary of the day we endured childbirth, because the two events are really so similar. They're painful, unthinkably messy and invoke a feeling of elation when they're over. So if you are the sort who decided to give birth in a hospital where there were professionals to supervise and clean up, you might want to do the same with your child's birthday party. Go anywhere: a sports place, an art place, the candy store, the park. A construction site with a porta-potty! I cannot overstate the intense tranquility of returning home to my ordinary mess after one of these events.

3. Bring another adult. There was this one year when I took a bunch of kids to laser tag and my little one got his eye sliced open and needed stitches and I had all these kids and there was a lot of blood and thank goodness my friend Maria was there and drove them all home. I've blocked out the rest, but you get the idea.

4. Have the party on the actual birthday: This is one thing I'm getting right for the very first time this year. I used to choose the Saturday closest to my child's birthday for his party. I'd have the Saturday party (suffering all manner of stress, hair loss and intestinal ailments alluded to above) and then a few days later on his actual birthday, he'd say, "So what are we doing for my birthday?" I'd scramble to find photos to refresh his memory, but to no avail. The party's long forgotten, the frosting's been fully metabolized and the gifts were already broken. His actual birthday felt like a letdown. Bring on round two: another cake, fresh balloons and the general merriment that can only be found at Party City.

5. Party favors can be anything. By the time those kids leave, they are so tired and strung out on sugar that they don't care what's in that goody bag. But I'm not saying you can skip it! Children over the age of two are programmed to expect entertainment, pizza and cake, followed by a bag of stuff offered as payment for having attended the party. They'll stand there

and wait, holding your gaze until you meet your end of the bargain. Don't prolong their departure by having to explain that you are too "green" to give them a bag of landfill.

My kid's party starts in an hour. I've got to go find some stuff to put in those goody bags. Any stuff will do.

Teenagers Prove You Can Simultaneously Know Everything and Nothing

Teenagers fool us with their size, vocabulary and swift mastery of new devices. They seem to be about the right shape to fit into the adult world. They drive cars. They know algebra. So it's always momentarily shocking to find out that they don't know how to address an envelope or operate a can opener.

My teenagers are the only people in my house who are as smart as my smart TV. I honestly have to enlist their help every time I want to change the channel. They know how to work Netflix, and they can figure out how to get WiFi anywhere in the world. And yet …

My son recently started a road trip by quickly clicking an address on his phone's GPS. He then drove to the exact right address in the wrong state. It's these little things that you'd never think to explain that turn out to be big things. When he was leaving, should I have added "Go to the right state!" to my standard "Make good choices!"?

My teenagers know pi to 20 decimal places, but they do not understand why keys matter. They use and discard their house keys like tissues. I sat dumbfounded as my husband explained to them the etymology of the word "key." The reason people refer to the most important part as the "key" part is because keys are really important. *Seriously*, I wondered, *Does this even need to be said? How could a person with the motor skills to operate a key not know this?*

They know all the elements on the periodic table. They can name every starting player on every team in the NBA. But they were surprised to learn that chicken, left on the counter overnight, goes bad. At some point facts like this become a matter of survival.

Of course some of this is just the teenage brain, designed like a sieve and with an incomplete prefrontal cortex. But it's also a lack of information. Their defense is simple and consistent: "I didn't know that was a thing." That explanation should find its way into a scientific journal.

I didn't know that was a thing. This phrase echoes in my mind, bringing me back to those hazy, soupy teen years when I could only see a few feet ahead of myself. My parents probably shook their heads a lot, but they didn't try to spoon-feed me facts. No one waved from the bus stop shouting, "Have a good day! Don't drink water from a still pond! Run in a zigzag if a bear chases you!" Everything I know I learned from cartoons or calamity.

There are a million things I never knew were a thing. When I was 19, I bought a used Volkswagen for $500. At the time I knew a lot about French literature and pretty much everything about William Faulkner. But I didn't know you needed to put oil in a car. No one had ever told me, so I didn't know that was a thing.

That same year I backpacked all over Europe with my passport in my back pocket. Now that I think of it, passports could be described as "key." I didn't know that was a thing either.

I can work myself into a panic thinking of all the things that my kids probably don't know. Don't drink soda and eat pop rocks, or your head will explode. Never put your drink down at a bar. A person who starts a sentence with "to be honest" isn't going to be. If you see the shoreline sink rapidly, run!

This must be why parents just stick to the basics: Look both ways before you cross the street, wash your hands, don't let the bedbugs bite.

The rest of it is going to be filled in along the way, an education provided not by us but by a series of small catastrophes that they'll likely survive.

Coming Home Empty-Handed
From the School Fair

I've just returned from the school fair. I am completely dehydrated, my feet hurt, and I am in possession of one partially mutilated cake that my son won at the cakewalk. My youngest son got his face painted, and I'm watching him casually transfer that paint to all of the upholstered surfaces of my home. If I had 15 percent less sugar in my system, I could get up and wash that face.

All that said, I consider it a pretty successful day because I got through the fair without acquiring a goldfish.

I have radar for innocuous things that are going to turn out to be my problem. I can see it in the eyes of the lady who is approaching me with a great idea for a fundraiser; I hear it in the voice of my son who's asking me for a shoebox for a school project. I knew that my husband's new juicer was going to be my problem before I got all 19 "hand wash only" pieces out of the box. After a month in my kitchen, a crime lab wouldn't be able to find a single one of his prints on that thing. That juicer is my problem. The goldfish from the school fair is no different.

I cringed as I watched other people's goldfish acquisitions replay themselves in front of me all day: the elated child running up to his parent, "I won a goldfish!" The word "won" is a bit of a stretch. For the price of one punch on your fair card, you get a chance to scoop a balloon out of a kiddy pool. If you get it, you get a fish. If you don't get it, you get a fish. This partially plays into our culture of sending everyone home a winner, but I suspect it has more to do with the fact that whoever is in charge of the goldfish station doesn't want to be schlepping 600 goldfish home at the end of the day. That's really an inordinate amount of flushing.

The parents groan. They know that this little goldfish brings with it a teaching moment about the circle of life. And that moment's coming soon because that plastic bag prisoner is probably going to be floating by cocktail hour. But they smile and congratulate their child, agreeing to carry that little bag around for the rest of the day. We lock eyes as we pass, nodding our condolences with a sarcastic, "Oh, I see your daughter won a fish too!" Echoes of "dead fish swimming" fill the halls.

If you don't have a floater in your baggie by the end of the fair, you've won a fish that lives for multiple years. (I have heard no stories of fair fish that live a few months; it's either hours or years.) This hearty fish is the one that becomes my problem, and I've had plenty. This fish survives any amount of neglect, extreme temperatures and an extended family vacation. This is the fish that lives long enough to actually finish the container of fish food that we bought on the way home from our first fair.

Of all the thankless things mothers take on, I think the weekly cleaning of the goldfish bowl takes the prize. The fundraiser raises money, and the juicer keeps my husband healthy, but I get nothing back from that fish. He doesn't wag his fin at me when I walk in the house. He doesn't know any tricks at all. I just watch as he circles the bowl with that impassive (and maybe insincere) kissy face. To be honest, I even get a little bored watching people swim.

Yes, my kids hit the cupcake room more times than I care to count and "won" multiple whoopee cushions today, but they somehow missed the fish station. My fishbowl is still safely packed away, so I've had a very successful day at the fair.

The Greatest Mother in the World

I saw a woman leaving the YMCA yesterday with a baby strapped to her chest, another slightly larger child in a stroller, and a three-year-old holding her hand. She was infested with small children. I stopped to watch. I wondered, *How in the world are they going to make it to their car? How is she going to cross the great abyss between where she is right now and bedtime?*

When they got close enough, I could hear that the three-year-old was trying to make a scene. I say "trying to make a scene" because he was waging war against his mother, and she was refusing to participate. With a steady gait and an even expression, she ignored him. It was the most spectacular moment in parenting I have ever seen. This woman, who I imagine lives in a shoe, should teach a seminar.

It seemed that I had walked in on the one-sided battle late. The three-year-old was saying, "You're so mean to me" over and over again. I tried to think back to all of the things I would have said in this situation when I had toddlers to defend myself against. "I'm mean??" I would have started. "You're the one who…" But she said nothing, and without a reaction from his mother, this kid was firing blanks.

He tried a new approach. "I'm freezing. I don't even have any pockets." To which his mother responded, "Oh, that's too bad. You should have brought a jacket with pockets." There was not a hint of sarcasm in her voice. She said this in the tone you would use to say, "I think I'm going to wear my blue sweater today." The cold weather was not going to turn into an emotionally charged subject either.

There before me was a new existential question of parenting: If a child has a fit in the parking lot and his mother doesn't react, did he really have a fit at all?

Pound for pound, a small child has more power in a public place than an adult. Small children have the advantage over the rest of us in that they are loud, and they are not self-conscious. It's a lethal combination. A temper tantrum at home can be tuned out. A temper tantrum on a full flight cannot.

For this reason, I bow my head out of respect when I encounter a two-year-old on an airplane. No one outside the cockpit has more control over how this flight's going to go than this pretty little creature with the Hello Kitty backpack. I smile at her panicked parents in solidarity. They try not to make eye contact, embarrassed because we are about to find out what a beast their child is. I pray that they're armed with markers, snacks and Benadryl.

A child hurling himself on the floor of the cereal aisle is exposing our worst insecurities to the eyes of strangers. Those eyes might actually be sympathetic, but in them we only see confirmation of the truth we've suspected all along: We're pretty much doing everything wrong. It was downright reckless of them to let us leave the hospital with a baby. Chances are we've ruined him already, so we might as well just give him the Froot Loops.

The key to our parking lot heroine's success is that she was decidedly not self-conscious. She was aware that I had stopped in my tracks to watch this scene, riveted. But in the same way she wasn't going to hand her power over to her three-year-old, she wasn't going to hand it over to me either. If I could go back in time and give my young-mother self one quality, it would be that ability to hold on to my power.

As they got in the car, the child threatened, "When we get home, I'm going to my room!" His mother replied, "I think that's a wonderful idea." Checkmate.

WHAT BOY MOMS KNOW

W hen I'm introduced to another mother of only boys, there are a few seconds of expectation. As if maybe we are going to have a secret handshake. Or maybe we are going to say, "Hey, are there black handprint marks all over your walls? Me too!"

Instead, we just nod our heads and exchange a little smile, knowing we are kindred spirits. Having boys leads to a set of personality traits, namely that you're not fussy and that you roll with the (actual) punches. If you have a bunch of boys, you've probably seen a femur up close, and you can get blood out of anything.

Mothers of boys are strangely laid back about property damage. In fact, property damage is to boy moms what frequent costume changes are to girl moms. A golf club through the drywall, a child through the drywall and a basketball game ending triumphantly with glass showering down from the ceiling lights. That's just what being a boy mom is. It's knowing the number of the window repair company by heart and not having to tell them your address when you call.

Boy moms buy eggs four dozen at a time. We're why they package 32 English muffins together at Costco. An English muffin with peanut butter on it will sate our starving boys for up to 25 minutes, enough time to boil up some macaroni and cheese or order a pizza. We are slightly afraid of our growing and starving brood, because their collective hunger comes at us with such force and frequency. I've been known to throw down a plate of bacon and run out of the room like a lion trainer fleeing the cage.

We have time for all this food shopping and prep because we do not shop for clothes. We do not meander through the mall, browsing the new spring fashions. We buy socks like we buy eggs, dozens at a time. When we need to buy clothes for our children, our shopping list reads "everything, the next size up." And that usually works out fine. We shop for ourselves, of course, though we don't really need to. Not one person in my house knows what kind of jeans I should be wearing this season. For this, I am particularly grateful.

The other, unspoken thing that bonds us boy moms is what we don't have: a daughter. Sometimes the fact that I don't have a daughter surprises me so much that I check myself like I'm patting my pockets for my keys. She's got to be around here somewhere, I have so much to tell her! All these hard-earned girl lessons just roll around my head, waiting for eager ears. She'd probably just roll her eyes anyway. *Really, Mom? What do you know about boys?*

Without a daughter, I wonder about the future of my stuff. Every year on Thanksgiving I try to get one of my sons excited about my mom's gravy boat. Every year someone asks if it wouldn't just be easier to serve the gravy out of the roasting pan on the stove. Easier? It would have been easier to just order a pizza, but that's not the point. It is my greatest hope that some-day they'll sit down to dinner with their own families (just having repaired their own drywall), see that gravy boat and get the point.

We boy moms won't go prom dress shopping. We won't pick the wedding venue. We won't be in the delivery room. We won't ever, ever sit on a toilet before thoroughly inspecting it first. But we will strive to raise kind, conscious, able young men. All of this is acknowledged when boy moms meet and exchange a little nod and a smile. The nod is for the food prep and the property damage. The smile is for all the rest: the sweetness of a little boy, and the way he grabs your heart with his dirty hands and never lets go.

CASE CLOSED ON THE MISSING SOCKS

There are many baffling questions we ask again and again, hoping that maybe in the afterlife their answers will be revealed to us. *Why are we here? Why can't time fly when we're not having fun? Where did my waist go?* And, of course, there is the eternal question of the missing socks. *Where, oh where, do they go?*

That last one's easy. They're all at my house.

There was a time when socks in my house were found in a sock drawer, in a hamper or on a pair of feet. Then I had children. There are now socks in every corner of my house. They are under couches, mixed in with toys and hanging off the fireplace grate. They are strewn on the stairs, as if there was a fire and everyone had to strip off their socks in order to speed their escape.

When I've collected and washed them all, they amount to a staggering pile of need-to-be-matched socks. We are a family of ten feet. I, for one, go through no more than one pair a day, mainly on principle. My husband ranges between one and two pairs. But the others — they don't exercise such self-control. It seems they need different socks for every activity, and if they make a sock-footed trip outside, they need a fresh pair upon their return. My kids take a lot of sock-footed trips outside each day.

It is not difficult to personify the sock pile. Mine actually has a pulse. It is a living, breathing, growing entity capable of doing anything but matching its own kind. Each week the Nike and Under Armour socks seem to be breeding and spawning a new race of socks that I have never seen before. There are argyle socks, Adidas socks and even pink socks in my pile. It's like Studio 54 in there.

These new, foreign socks arrive at my house in a steady stream. I blame the trampoline. Every child that comes to my house takes off his shoes and runs out to the trampoline in their socks. The mud immediately renders those socks squishy, and the kids discard them like confetti all over my backyard. It's actually quite whimsical the way the socks dangle from the shrubs. The child leaves with just his shoes, deciding he would rather ride bareback than touch those muddy socks again. In this way, my sock inventory has risen by at least two socks every day for eight years.

Being the designated sorter of all these socks can be soul crushing. I imagine my parents sending me off to college and hoping that my life would amount to some higher purpose than this. The black dress socks in particular could make you go blind. Some have gold toes, some have wider ribs, some are longer than others. Holding them up to a bare bulb in my basement, I wonder, *If i can't tell the difference why do they even need to match at all?*

Like Cinderella, I dream of a way out. Like Cinderella, I do not act. I'm waiting for someone to rescue me. In the meantime, if you want your socks back, you know where they are.

This Just in — My Kid Got a Job!

Raising kids isn't cheap. At first it's just the basics like shelter, clothing and food, but it quickly spirals out of control into music classes, their own seat on an airplane and many, many pairs of subtly different cleats. The first time I saw the price of six weeks of summer camp, I gasped and (briefly) considered hanging out with them myself.

Then there's a point in the tween-to-teen transition when kids need actual cash. Their social lives no longer happen on the playground. They meet up with their friends at and around places that sell pizza and snacks, and without a few bucks, it's technically considered loitering. They don't need a lot, just a five or a ten (*please, Mom*). It was at this stage in my oldest son's life that I started to feel like there was a hole in my pocket.

Which brings me to my big news: My kid got a job. Like for money. I'm trying to let this inevitable but totally unanticipated event sink in. At the most basic level, I'm blown away that he's going to be spending the day doing something that I'm not paying for. It's like he's going to free daycare and coming home with a pocket full of minimum wage.

That's not even the best part. While he's at this place (for free, plus salary), he's actually going to learn what $20 means. He already knows what it buys: it's eight slices of pizza, a trip to the movies or the price of the basketball he just lost. Frequently, it's just one slice of pizza and a soda, the change from which gets crumbled in his pocket only to be found and kept by me on laundry day. Any which way, a twenty goes pretty fast.

What he doesn't yet understand is where that $20 comes from. A person with a job quickly learns that a trip to the movies costs nearly three hours of work. Specifically, he's going to have to fetch beach chairs and umbrellas in the hot sun for three hours in order to go to one air-conditioned movie with popcorn. This watershed learning experience marks the exact moment when people get a little pickier about the movies they see.

The $20 lesson is one of the many, many things that you can't teach your kids through talking. I tell them about pre-tax dollars and social security contributions, and they give me that look that I give people when they talk about grandchildren. *I get the concept, but how is this ever going to apply to me?* Only the experience of holding that precious first paycheck in your hand and thinking, "Wait. That's it?" can teach you what $20 really is.

My mom did not have a hole in her pocket, so I got my first summer job at fourteen. In 1984 we weren't bound by things like working papers or the truth. I walked into a local store and asked if they were hiring for the summer. When asked my age, I replied, "How old do I have to be to get the job?" I thought it was a fair enough question. In this way I worked through high school summers folding sweaters, then scooping ice cream and eventually answering phones. These are all skills that I brought with me into adulthood.

It was the office jobs, filing stuff, that made me really think about the future. Cooped up under the fluorescent lights, breathing the recirculated air and watching the clock move backward, I realized that money isn't easy to get. I started to understand how much of someone's life is spent working and the importance of finding a job that captures your interest. I had no idea what I wanted to do with my life, but I knew it wasn't putting other people's paperwork in alphabetical order.

He's going to learn a lot about life this summer. Oh! And the best part? They're going to feed him lunch.

How I Got This Crazy Tan

Like everyone else on earth, summer meant everything to me when I was a kid. I can still remember the feeling of the last day of school when the nuns made us take our desks outside and wash them. That hint of sunshine and the welcome splash of water in my saddle shoes was a preview of things to come. Soon I'd be staring into the wide-open space of summer: no have-tos and no ankle-sock tan lines.

My mom had a rule about my partaking in one activity every summer. During the summer that I was thirteen, that activity was taking tennis lessons. I know, this may come as a shock to those of you who have seen me play tennis. *Is it possible*, you wonder, *that this person has ever had the benefit of professional instruction?* Of course not. By "taking tennis lessons," I mean that my mom dropped me off at the tennis courts on her way to work, and I waited until she'd left the parking lot before hopping on the Wilshire Boulevard bus to the beach. Once there, rotating the position of my towel according the movement of the sun was my only real have-to. She never noticed that my tan lines looked more like Baywatch than Wimbledon.

Later, when I got my first full-time job, complete with health insurance and the makings of an ulcer, they told me I was entitled to two weeks vacation. Two weeks sounded pretty good for, say, Christmas vacation, but I was alarmed to find out that they meant for the whole year. And then I found out that those two weeks didn't kick in until after I'd worked a whole year straight. That was the first year I had no tan lines and a vitamin D deficiency.

So when I landed the stay at home mom gig, I figured I had it made. I'd be on a kids' schedule with summers and spring break! All of that childhood freedom would be mine again. Long, lazy, sun-drenched days, lemonade in a crystal pitcher on a porch. Me, in a white sundress that would somehow stay white after a whole day of frolicking. Being a mom is practically all vacation if you think about it.

I realized my miscalculation right away. But I still try to steal back that summer feeling, that impending freedom. I decide which book I'm going to read first and outline elaborate writing projects. I buy new sunscreen and identify a spot on the beach where my blood pressure will plummet. This dream feels so obtainable, all I have to do to get there is drive my kids around a bit.

That task looks a bit like this: I drop one child at camp at 8 o'clock, come home to feed another and drive him to camp at 9 o'clock. I come home in time to eat breakfast myself and consider starting my summertime reverie but realize there's not enough time before I need to wake and feed the oldest one whose job starts at 11. Ah, time to start my day … though the 8 o'clock kid needs to be picked up some days at noon, some days at 2. Throw in a 3 o'clock pick up for the 9 o'clock kid, 5:30 dinner and a basketball game at 6:30 …

And I've just explained why moms wander around for most of July saying, "I feel like summer hasn't really started yet." Or why people keep asking me, "Where have you been?" *In my car! You?*

I've also just explained my peculiar tan lines. I have a driver's tan, just on my left arm and the left side of my face. It's half a tan, something out of a Batman movie, which seems about right because moms get half a summer vacation. Half good and half driving.

The hard truth, as I am finally coming to accept it, is that being a mom is really just like any other job. You don't get three months of vacation. The have-tos remain and sometimes multiply, so the best you can do is just enjoy the hard work that summer eliminates: finding people's mittens, shoveling the driveway, talking about homework and avoiding volunteer jobs.

At this stage of life, the only way to create vacation is to actually take it, to pull my children out of their lives and place them somewhere where none of us has any have-tos. I am writing this from my actual, legit summer vacation, which I define as seven days in a place where I do not have access to a car. And I'm trying to turn the right side of my face to the sun, just to even things out.

A One-Step Guide to Packing Your
Kid's Stuff for Vacation — Don't!

When you give birth to a child, that child entrusts you with a thousand small tasks that are necessary for his survival and comfort. It's important to remember that these tasks are on loan, that we need to eventually give them back to the child for our own survival and comfort. The bathing thing reverts back to them. The shoe-tying thing reverts back to them. I delight in each of these milestones, but none has felt better than letting my kids pack their own stuff for vacation.

I should have learned my lesson when I was first married, the time my husband was running late and asked me to pack his bag for a wedding. Instead of a suit, I accidentally grabbed his tuxedo, and he spent the weekend overdressed, annoyed and repeatedly mistaken for a waiter. On the bright side, he has never asked me to pack for him again. I believe this is what they refer to as a self-correcting problem.

But when I had kids, I found myself once again in the capacity of packing other people's suitcases full of all the wrong stuff. I would spend the whole week at grandma's explaining why I chose to pack the T-shirt with the too-tight sleeves, the underwear with the grabby liner and the book that he finished two weeks ago. Or answering questions like, "You didn't bring my headphones? Who goes on vacation without headphones?" *I don't know. Me? Henry David Thoreau?*

Whoever coined the phrase "no good deed goes unpunished" was certainly up all night with a child who couldn't sleep because his mother had packed the scratchy pajamas. When it comes to packing for your family, please follow this simple rule: Don't do it.

My failure as a packer stems from the fact that I'm neither a professional valet nor a mind reader. One person's mind is not broad enough to grasp all the nuances of another person's complex system of sorting and choosing. Personally, I own 20 T-shirts, all with different purposes. I have some for exercising, some that don't leave the house and some that are good under a sweater but should never be exposed to direct sunlight. I could hire a curator to come and catalog my T-shirts, and she still wouldn't be able to pack for me.

And jeans? As if. I have many pairs, and each is slightly different in terms of size, length, wash and waist height. I choose jeans based on event venue, height of attendees, phase of the moon and whether I'm going to be standing or sitting. In fact, if there's any chance I'm going to be sitting on a barstool, I only have two pairs of jeans that would prevent me from offending the people behind me. I am the only person alive who knows which two those are.

If I threw caution to the wind and asked my kids to pack me a pair of jeans, I'd end up having a conversation like this:

"Why would you pack those jeans?"

"I don't know. You just said 'jeans.'"

"Those jeans haven't fit me since 1987."

"Then why do you even have them?"

"I liked 1987."

I pack my own stuff primarily because I don't want to have to explain what was so great about 1987.

I want to offer a metaphor here about my children packing their bags as a part their learning to think ahead and gather what they need to embark on life's great journey. But that's really not what this is about. My kids' packing their own bags is about honoring the basic concept of vacation: taking a break from what you normally do the other 51 weeks of the year. If I'm fielding complaints and looking for other people's stuff, I'm pretty much just doing my day job.

Letting your kids pack for themselves may seem a bit like letting the inmates run the asylum, so it's important to protect yourself. I type up a deliberately vague list and print a copy for each of them: 4 pairs of shorts, 4 T-shirts, 5 pairs of socks, 5 pairs of underwear. ... Then for insurance I add, "Anything else you may want to bring."

I pack one copy of the list in my bag for reference. When they say, "Mom, I don't have any extra socks," I produce the document and counter with, "Oh darn, let's look and see if that was on the list. ..." Sure, that kid's going to spend a week in the one pair of socks that he left the house in, but see how it's not my problem?

My Dishwasher and Me

S ometimes the deepest friendships take a while to solidify. They don't seem obvious at first. Maybe you have different interests, different backgrounds. Maybe one of you is a human being and the other is a dishwasher. Whatever the barriers are, they can often fall away once you spend a lot of time with someone. My dishwasher and I are constantly interacting, and over the past several years, I'd say we've reached a certain level of intimacy.

Fun fact: she's not original to the house. When I bought my house, it came with a dishwasher that spoke 17 languages. I'm sure you know someone like this. She was kind of braggy about it, shifting from one language to the next with no prompting by me. Some days when she was speaking some Slavic language, I'd pretend like it was fun. I'd act playful like I do at Ikea where everything is an inexpensive and unnecessarily complicated puzzle. But on the days when she was Japanese, I sort of felt like the whole thing was rigged against me and I was letting her down. Sometimes friendships just get to be too much work.

And to be honest she needed way too much affirmation, letting out a big clang every time she finished a cycle. I'd roll my eyes, *Geez, do you want me to throw you a parade?* If I didn't know the 50-minute cycle was over because 50 minutes had passed, I was reminded by the clang and then by a display panel boasting "Finished!" Or "Finito!" Or "Päättynyt," which is actually the Finnish word for finished. It was just too much.

I feel bad saying this, but I was glad when she died.

Her replacement is the best, and it wasn't long until we became close friends. She's German, but she speaks English, which helps us find common ground. After the coffee maker, she's the first appliance I reach for in the morning. We like to play a game where I press go on the coffee maker and see if I can unload all the dishes before the coffee's ready. Some days I nail it, some days I fall short. Those failed days are usually the ones when there's Tupperware on the top shelf, and I have to hand wipe those infuriating drops of water off the plastic.

This is when we argue. *Why,* I need to know, *can she dry everything but the Tupperware?* It's like she purposefully directs her heat to avoid it. She's defiant about this, providing no real answers but reminding me that I'm slowly poisoning my family by putting that stuff in the dishwasher anyway. Touché, Fraulein. Touché.

After all, I respect her and her work ethic. And not to judge, but I find it kind of offensive the way some people coddle their dishwashers by wiping their dishes completely clean before loading. It's kind of like taking a strep test before you go see the doctor. You might as well just come out and call him incompetent.

Not me. I scrape the big chunks into the trash and let her do what she does best. This backfires of course with things like mozzarella cheese and chia seeds. She has a sensitive digestive system and these things seem to, well, clog her up. Sorry if that was too personal. That bit of information probably wasn't mine to share.

We touch base every day, but our quality time really happens on the weekends. Everyone's home, everyone's hungry and everyone likes to approach each drink with a new glass. The weekends are when her little spinning arm gets an ironman's workout, and by Monday morning, she needs a rest.

You'd think my family would resent this relationship, as much time as we spend together. But no, the truth is that they really give us our space. My kids, in particular, like to give her privacy. They approach her with a dirty mug in hand, slowly open her door just a crack to check things out. If, God forbid, her contents are clean, they slam that door, leave the mug on the counter and flee the scene. It's cute how they don't want to take away from our special time.

Raising Losers

We parents go to a lot of trouble to make sure our kids win — we hire tutors, we re-write their papers, we finish their sentences. We even condition them to expect to win by making sure that every six-year-old who sets foot on a soccer field leaves with a trophy. If our kids are bad losers, it's not their fault — it's just that they haven't had any practice.

The thing is, losing isn't really that big of a deal if you've done it a few times. I've had so much experience with losing that I barely even notice it anymore. There's the initial disappointment, the cathartic "it's not fair" and then the regrouping. You look around and see that the world is still spinning, that you are still the same person you were before the game. And you move on. A person whose life is one long undefeated season doesn't know how to move through that sacred cycle of falling and getting back up.

So if you want your kids to have some experience in losing, try games that you can only win after losing a few times. One of my favorites is called "The Morning Game." The object of the game is to get out of the house with all of the stuff you will need for the next six hours. (I didn't say it was easy.) If you forget your lunch/homework/library book, you lose. But, as a consolation prize, you learn life skills like begging for half a sandwich, making up excuses and negotiating with the librarian. The player is disqualified from this game the instant his mother arrives at school with the forgotten items. The player who wins for five consecutive days has mastered a game that he will be playing every single day for the rest of his life.

Another good one is called "Where Are My Cleats?" It involves two players, the younger of whom is looking for his cleats. The older player knows where they are (having previously lost the game called "Who's

Gonna Clean Up This House Every Day?"), but pretends not to. The older player keeps saying, "I don't know, where do you keep them?" until the younger player finds them and decides that having a dedicated spot for the cleats would be a good idea. Both players lose during the first few rounds, being late for practice and managing the crankiness of the other. But in the end, both will win.

There's a part of me that wants to turn my kids into serious losers. The kind that know how to say "Sorry I'm late." and "Sorry I forgot." The kind that can deal with running extra laps and leaving the library without a new book. Medical science has proven that it's impossible to die from such losses, but be warned — side effects may include dizziness, nausea and growing up.

The Siri Relationship

I enjoy my one-sided relationship with Siri. I press a button when I need something, and she is always there with the correct answer or a promise of a reminder. In return, she asks nothing of me. I don't have to respond to a single one of her needs. Actually, I've never even bothered to ask what they are. Our relationship is 100 percent about me. And I don't feel that bad about it because, at some point, we're all Siri to somebody.

The Siri dynamic happens during a time when a relationship is off balance. One person takes on the role of the Asker and the other becomes the Responder. The Asker reaches out when she needs something, and the Responder's job is to always be there. Assuming an adequate level of self-esteem, you decide to be Siri for someone because you really love them. And because you know it's going to be temporary.

For example, you often have a Siri relationship with a friend who is in crisis. That friend calls you with her problems, and there's no other pretext for the conversation. If she's going through a divorce or a serious illness, that topic trumps whatever you've got going on. Your friend in crisis doesn't want to hear that you're annoyed because you just drove all the way to the market to get ground beef for meatballs, and all they had was ground turkey. If she frequently forgets to ask how you are, it's just to protect herself from this ground turkey conversation. It's basic crisis survival.

Increasingly, I have the Siri relationship with my older children. Teenagers, by definition, are people in crisis. For my particular teenagers, the crises generally revolve around food. They press a button to text me from their rooms: "When's dinner?" or "I'm starving!" or the ever-important "Did you buy bananas?" And I respond. This dynamic seems as natural to me as their learning to walk and talk. It's just part of the process, and it's temporary.

I know this imbalance is temporary because my mother was Siri to me during my teenage years and beyond. I would only call her from college when I was knee deep in a problem, back when a phone call was a major event that cost money and happened in a public hallway. I would regale her with my troubles and my resulting needs. She would respond. And then the following week, after she'd wrung out her hands in worry, and I'd forgotten about the whole thing, we'd talk again. "Oh, that?" I'd tell her, "It's fine … I passed the test," "We got back together" or "The doctor said it was nothing. …"

See, here's the thing: You don't follow up with Siri. If you ask her for the closest Chinese restaurant, you don't text later to tell her how the Moo Shu was. You just wait till you're hungry again and send out a new request.

When I had children of my own, I elevated my mom from Siri to Saint. I saw with newly human eyes her humanness, felt with a tired heart how tired she must have been all the time. How did she pull off Christmas every year? How did she work full time and put together such elaborate dinners? How was she always wearing makeup? And so I started calling just to ask how she was. I wanted to know how work was going and what she was reading. Did she have plans Saturday night, and if so, what was she going to wear? I started downplaying my own drama in favor of a cute story about one of my kids. We were back in balance.

Sometimes the most valuable thing you can do for a person is to be Siri for a while, to stand still while they are spinning. Teenagers, in particular, seem to need to know that we are planted firmly in place, texting distance away (and preferably looking frumpy). They don't need to know about our friendships, our ups and downs and our worries while they sort through their own.

I'm grateful for all the times people have been Siri to me. And as a show of my gratitude, I've stopped asking the actual Siri to call me "Foxy." She's never complained about it, of course, but I don't want to push my luck.

Welcome to My Midlife Crisis

I'm relieved to announce that my midlife crisis has come to an un-eventful conclusion. I have emerged untouched by an obscure tattoo, a tennis pro or the leather seats of a new sports car. I didn't even start wearing cutoff shorts with boots (you're welcome). There should be a ceremony to mark the ending of this stage of life, a Hallmark card at a minimum.

I'd outline for you the progression of my midlife crisis if it wasn't equal parts boring and personal. Let's just say it started the day I saw "Crazy, Stupid, Love" and realized that I was supposed to relate to the middle-aged Julianne Moore character, not the twenty-something Emma Stone charac-ter. And it ended with the realization that the Julianne Moore stage of life is actually pretty great. What it lacks in excitement and angst, it makes up for in joy and appreciation. Ryan Gosling would have started to get on my nerves anyway. Maybe.

I've been surprised to learn that people engaged in a midlife crisis seek each other out. At first I worried that I was starting to look a little like Dr. Phil because people came out of the woodwork to confide in me about their crises. Several times in the past year I've asked someone, "How's it going?" only to get the reply "I'm having a midlife crisis." Recently, a colleague began a work-related call with, "Before we start, you should know I'm having a midlife crisis." The shock value ran out pretty quickly. I started telling everyone to take a number and hunker down.

Some women dealing with their midlife crisis tell me about the careers they left behind and that feeling of financial powerlessness that comes with having spent a decade or two caring for children. Others tell me about their marriages, that disconnected feeling that begs questions like "What happened to us?" and "What are we going to talk about when the kids leave?" From both men and women I hear the question "What now?" more than anything.

By the time you hit midlife, there's a good chance that you've been doing what you're currently doing for a while. I'd be unloading my dishwasher for the third time on a Saturday and think, *I should really be in France.* I mean, I've explored the whole dishwasher thing. I load it, I unload it. I get it. *What now?*

The midlife crisis is preceded by decades of running at full speed, chasing stuff like promotions and fertility and real estate. When we finally have some subset of what we set out to achieve, we are shocked to find that what we've really been doing is amassing a big pile of responsibilities. We can't just pick up and move to France anymore. We've got too much stuff.

But there is a way through it. I've seen people look at the next 50 years and decide that there are things from their youth that they actually can get back without abandoning the life they've made. Those things are a really satisfying answer to "What now?" and are often what we loved doing when we were young. A friend of mine is a very talented drummer turned Wall Streeter who, at midlife, has gotten his band back together. He recently invited us to his home to listen to them play, and we were all transported to a younger, freer time. I was inspired. And because it was mid-life, the beer was imported and the hors d'oeuvres were passed. As my husband noted, everyone there was on drugs, but this time it was Lipitor and Viagra. It was still cool.

The common theme here is the desire to reach back to the excitement of the possibilities of youth. We want to feel like we still have it all ahead of us. Behind us is falling in love for the first time, naturally blond hair and getting out of bed in the morning without noticing how your back feels.

But ahead of us is knowing who we are and maybe having a little more free time to explore that.

So I guess I'm not 24 anymore, and Ryan Gosling's probably not going to fix me a complicated cocktail and fall in love with me. I bet Julianne Moore's doing something a little more my speed tonight anyway.

In September, the Devil's in the Details

My apologies in advance to anyone who makes plans with me this month. There's an 80 percent chance I'm not going to show up. Likewise to anyone who invites my kids to a birthday party, relies on me for carpool or asks me to perform any kind of simple task. Like someone who's just arrived in New York City for the first time, I can't keep up with the pace of the new things being thrown at me. It's September, and I do not have my head screwed on straight yet.

As an illustration, let me play for you the best track on my "September's Greatest Screw-Ups" album: In 2006, at 9 a.m. on a Monday, I was in the parking lot of the grocery story when my phone rang. "Where are you?" asked the voice on the other end. I get this question all the time in September, so my answer was ready: "Why? Where am I supposed to be?" It turns out that this was the morning of the Kindergarten class coffee, and it also turns out that I had volunteered to bring all the food for said class coffee. I assured the hostess that I was on my way and raced into the store to buy all the carbs they had. Miraculously, I arrived at the party just 15 minutes late, a bit out of breath but seeming like I had everything under control. That is, until I removed my jacket to reveal to everyone in attendance that I was still wearing my pajamas.

In this way, the whole month of September seems kind of like a recurring nightmare. I am either a day late, a day early, or not there at all. I'll arrive at a cocktail party with a clipboard and at back-to-school night with a bottle of wine. And the reason for my disorientation isn't that I'm too overcommitted and busy. Who isn't overcommitted and busy? The dysfunction of September is that it looks like all the other months, but all the tiniest details have been changed.

If you're not paying attention, you're lost: library books are now due on Wednesdays; pick-up is at the other playground; the spelling words that had to be copied three times on Monday nights into a blue marble notebook now have to be copied four times on Tuesdays into a black marble notebook. They've even tweaked the cafeteria payment system, so I apologize if your kids end up buying my kids' lunch until I've mastered that in October.

It's the small details like these, the ones that can easily slip under the radar, that are my undoing. Success in the parenting business hinges almost entirely on one's ability to put the details on autopilot. We rely on the routine as the framework for the chaos. It's meatballs on Monday, basketball on Tuesday, piano on Wednesday. September is the month of reprogramming yourself to know who needs to be where, when, and with what supplies in a world that has shifted almost imperceptibly.

To add insult to injury, this September the high school and middle school are dismissing the students five minutes earlier every day. I'm pretty sure they're just messing with me. I will pick my kids up at 2:32 instead of the (equally arbitrary) 2:37 that I'd spent a previous September getting used to. There is a logical reason for this change that smart people seem to understand, but I am not yet in the know. Maybe next year they'll pick up the high school and move it six inches to the left.

THE TIME WARP OF BACK-TO-SCHOOL NIGHT

The cool kids are hanging by the lockers, laughing and talking a little too loud. The nerds are in the classroom early, eager to shake hands with the teacher and nab the seats in the front row. The girls are put together in skinny jeans, heels and blown-out hair. Obviously, this is back-to-school night, and these are the parents of actual high schoolers.

Back-to-school night for high school is dramatically different than it is at the elementary school. When you go to the little kids' school, you are acutely aware of your status as an adult. You sit in teeny tiny chairs and look through the "artwork" that your child has left for you. The teacher talks about how he's going to teach your kid to do stuff that you already know how to do. It's adorable how they're growing up, isn't it?

In contrast, back-to-school night at the high school makes you feel like a kid. I wander from class to class with no clue as to where I'm going. The traffic in the halls is so socially overwhelming that I find myself saying hello to everyone like I'm running for Student Council president. Skinny Jeans walks by me and flips her hair without saying hello. I wonder what that means. *Did I say the wrong thing? Did I say the right thing but to the wrong person, and it got back to her?*

I am in a time warp, and I've brought everyone with me. That guy who's texting in class, he was a note passer. That lady who's writing down every word the teacher says (even the jokes), she was the valedictorian. The jock in the back row is stretching because he had a really hard practice today. And look, he's married to a cheerleader.

And just like in high school, half the time I have no clue what the teachers are talking about. I walk into biology, and the teacher has an assignment for us on the board. "Record your inferences about these photos." *Look, lady, I didn't come here to do homework. You can't make me.* One photo looks like a bunch of colors and the other looks like a feather. I write that down, grudgingly. She starts her presentation by telling us the answer. I wasn't even close. I swear, just like high school.

When it's time for our break, I hit the cafeteria and am relieved to find my BFF. She seems relieved to find me too, and we move to a safe corner.

It's loud and crowded, and the popular girls are selling things behind a folding table, somehow already in a club. Skinny Jeans is there and looks sublimely happy. I have a feeling she feels like she's back in high school too.

I am happy when the bell rings and I can go to English. This woman speaks my language. I sit in the very front of the class (I guess that settles it, I'm a nerd), and my gaze tells her how much I love her and every book she's teaching and how much I want to be her when I grow up. Even though she's 30. I leave without saying hello, however, because I don't trust myself to be cool about it.

I go to more classes, each eight minutes long. Calculus, as it turns out, has very few numbers and is too complicated for the teacher to explain to us. I'm a little grateful. The bell rings again, and we check our schedules to figure out where our next class is. I have gym, so I instinctively run through my handy list of female problems that disarm male gym coaches. But then it hits me, I'm a grown up. I can just go home.

I'm Over the School Photo

When I had my first son, someone gave me one of those School Days photo frames to house all the school pictures I would collect over the years. It has twelve openings for photos from K through 11, and then a big celebratory photo for a senior portrait. I tend to be fairly goal oriented, so I liked the idea of having a way to visually track my progress while my kids go through school.

In reality, that frame is the most depressing thing I own. And I don't just mean the dwindling empty spaces that show me how many years I have left, like an X'ed-off calendar on a prisoner's wall. The depressing part is the photos themselves, my kids against an artificial background looking like they're under duress. If I wanted a collection of 13 awkward photos of my kids smiling nervously at a stranger, I'd just wait for the mug shots to roll in.

I imagine that school photos made sense many, many years ago. My parents and grandparents were seldom photographed except at school or at their own weddings. They did not live in a culture where parents watched every school play through the back of their smartphones. And they certainly didn't turn their cameras on themselves to commemorate every social gathering, every meal, every outfit change. In a pre-selfie world, I can see why school photos were necessary to commemorate the passage of a year. I'm not sure we need them now.

At last count, I have nearly a zillion photos of my kids. There are so many that I seldom go to the trouble of printing one out and putting it in a frame. My favorites feature my kids looking like kids: outside, laughing, a little dirty. When Future Me gets around to printing out the best of these photos and putting them into carefully assembled scrapbooks, I'm pretty sure the annual school photo won't even make the cut.

With your first child, you get sort of excited about their being professionally photographed. When the order form comes home, you pick the "Package A" that costs $54, the one that includes the 8x10 and six 3x5s and enough wallet-sized photos for all of your friends. Because, really, who doesn't want to stuff her wallet full of photos of other people's kids? You maybe spring for the retouching, the personalization on the back, and the refrigerator magnet so you are sure that the photo ends up in multiple rooms.

Smartly, the photo company asks you to commit to this purchase before you actually see the photo. Your kids are so cute — how could they take a bad photo? The picture day photos of my children are honestly the worst photos that they take all year. "Sit on this stool, lean a little forward, tilt your head up toward the ceiling while keeping your eyes on me, while I comb your hair in a direction it's never gone before. ... Say cheese!" They often end up with an expression that suggests someone just punched them in the kidneys.

I wised up by the time my second son went to school. I ordered "Package Z," which is maybe $15 and consists of an individual photo for us to laugh about and the class photo. (I have to admit, I love the class photo. It feels like a historical document. I keep them in case one of my sons ends up marrying the girl in the third row or in case the kid making the funny face ever runs for President.)

One year when my youngest was in preschool, I brought him to class on picture day, and the teacher gasped when she saw him in his customary Yankee t-shirt and basketball shorts. "Oh no!" she cried. "I forgot to remind you it was picture day!" I knew darn well it was picture day, and I thought he looked pretty good. I wasn't about to add a starchy collar and a necktie to the awkwardness of the event. I didn't spring for the refrigerator magnet that year either.

KEEPING UP WITH THE FOOD NETWORK

B ecause I lost control of the clicker about a decade ago, I spend November watching a lot of football and a lot of Food Network.

My husband flips back and forth between the NFL and home-style cornbread stuffing, mesmerized by the way these TV chefs prepare elaborate meals in perpetually clean kitchens. I suspect he thinks an onion comes finely chopped and in a perfectly sized glass bowl. I don't want to burst his bubble, but as Thanksgiving nears, and I find that none of my vegetables chop themselves, I'd like to see a little more reality on this reality TV network.

Every year the food celebrities invite us into their shiny kitchens and urge us to take it up a notch. Why not make a mosaic out of fresh herbs under the skin of your turkey? Why not use a blowtorch on your apple pie? Or my personal favorite: Why not take three different kinds of birds, debone them and tie them all together, separated by a thin layer of stuffing? This, the hauntingly named "Turducken," signals to me the fall of civilization.

Just for once, I'd like to see the army of choppers, measurers and cleaners that seem to disappear just before the cameras roll. If you're telling me to add my 40 cloves of garlic, I'd like you to acknowledge just how long it takes to peel 40 cloves of garlic. I'd like a bunch of kids to run into the kitchen tracking dirt and blood and Fritos while you're slicing the pancetta for your stuffing. I'd like to see Ina Garten look kind of annoyed because she just found out that she has a vegetarian coming for Sunday dinner. I'd like, just once, to see Giada De Laurentiis stand there with her 24-inch waist and eat an entire portion of her cheesy mashed potatoes. We can see you, Giada. We can see you.

But what I'd really like to know is exactly what Bobby Flay's been up to behind the scenes. In fact, I'd pay $69.95 to see the fight that preceded his most recent show where he invited us into his kitchen to watch him prepare breakfast in bed for his wife. "Shhh," he reminded us, "she's still sleeping upstairs." He started by making homemade sausage and biscuits. By homemade, I mean he started with meat bits and flour. Then he made scrambled eggs, homemade doughnuts and homemade strawberry jelly. From actual strawberries.

How early do you have to wake up (or how late does your wife have to sleep?!) for you to make homemade sausage for breakfast? Pretty early, I'm guessing, and Bobby confided to the audience that he always makes this breakfast when he's "in trouble." Trouble? What did he do? This isn't like an I-forgot-our-anniversary apology. He actually carries this stuff up on a tray with a cocktail of tangerine juice and gin to wash it down. I'm hard pressed to think of what my husband could possibly do to make him feel like he needed to wake me up with gin. I had to watch the show all the way through to the credits because I was sure the police would be cuffing him at any minute.

The only thing I can think of is that he deep fried a turkey and burned down the garage. I have been mentally preparing myself for this eventuality ever since my husband first watched the "Deep Fried Turkey Marathon" on this evil network. Deep frying a turkey appeals to my husband in a visceral way. And I get it. The only thing missing from this, the fattest day of the year, is something fried. It's only a matter of time before I own a deep fryer large enough for a 30-pound roaster, and I'm pretty sure we're not insured for what ensues. At least I have breakfast in bed to look forward to.

The Golden Ticket

There are times in life when fate smiles on you in an unexpected way, and you wonder if you've done something wonderful to deserve it or if it's just good luck. Maybe you find yourself upgraded on a long flight. Maybe your child becomes a professional athlete and buys you a condo in Palm Beach. Or the ultimate: you are invited to be a guest at Thanksgiving dinner. No ironing linens, no greasy roaster. It is the gift of time and tranquility, the true golden ticket.

I have been in this coveted position twice in my adult life. On both occasions, I have rekindled my childhood love of Thanksgiving, tasting cranberry sauce as if for the first time. One particular year, I sat with my feet up in front of my hostess' blazing fire and thought: *If I play my cards right I can do this again next year.* But that's the catch, you have to play your cards right. And I have to assume that, maybe a bit giddy with free time and a clean kitchen, I didn't play them right, because I wasn't invited back.

I've hosted a lot of times. We have very little local family, so we always invite friends for Thanksgiving. I spend the first half of the year compiling a mental list of friends who may not have big Thanksgiving plans, and then I determine which ones I'd like to spend two weeks cooking dinner for. If you've been to my house for Thanksgiving dinner, you know two things: what it's like to eat a mediocre meal and that I really, really like you. I have, after all, given you the golden ticket.

So if it happens to you this year, if fate smiles upon you and you are invited to someone's house for Thanksgiving, please benefit from my mistakes and consider these suggestions to improve your odds of winning again next year:

1. Go to any length necessary to conceal the fact that you purchased the ONE thing the hostess asked you to bring to dinner. If you have to bring your own pie plate to the bakery and pay the guy extra to bake the apple pie in it, do so. If your savvy hostess suspects something, claim he gave you the recipe, and you've been peeling apples (that you picked yourself) all day. To be on the safe side, make a small incision in your left hand as proof.

2. Do not regale your hostess with stories of what you and your family did all day. Do not mention how Jimmy enjoyed the parade, do not comment on how beautiful the leaves were when you went for a run, and (I shouldn't have to say this) under no circumstances, are you to mention a nap. Your hostess woke up at 3 a.m. to get the turkey in the oven and was on her hands and knees cleaning up the brine she spilled all over the kitchen floor until 4 a.m. She did not get a nap. She has spent two weeks dusting, polishing and ironing her grandmother's good things. She's been to Costco and six different supermarkets and has tweaked her back from all the hauling. If you've had a manicure in the past ten days, keep it to yourself.

3. If you endured any traffic on your way to dinner, don't complain about it. When you mention the word "traffic," all your hostess hears is that you were sitting and listening to music for a couple of hours. Because she has been either standing or scrubbing since 3 a.m., she's unlikely to be sympathetic. And she may well be holding a knife.

4. Wear sensible shoes that suggest you plan to stand in front of the sink for a few hours after dinner. Your red-soled Louboutin's will play like a cape in a bullring if they are kicked up after dinner.

Ticket holders, take this advice to heart. And if you still end up hosting next year, carefully consider the worthiness of your invitees. Or just to be sure, invite me. I'll bring a pie.

OLD FRIENDS

I recently visited my childhood friend Valerie and found myself in fits of laughter like when we were 12. Being with her, things were funny in a way that they hadn't been in a long time. Every idiotic situation paralleled a more idiotic high school situation. If it didn't, it was something right out of "Valley Girl," which we decided in 1983 was the best movie ever.

My only explanation for all this laughing is that there is intrinsic relief in old friendships. In the presence of old friends, you don't have to keep selling the crazy notion that you've got it all together. Why bother putting up a front for a person who's seen you with a perm and a Flashdance sweatshirt? She remembers when life as a welder-turned-stripper seemed oddly appealing to you both. Your old friend knows you deep down; there's no place to hide.

Valerie and I have never been out of touch. But before this visit, it was more of a checking-in friendship, with status updates on major life events.

After our four days of laughing, I have spoken to her pretty much every day. I can't seem to let it go. We are back where we were as teenagers, in the middle of a conversation that lasted a decade. It's counterintuitive but true that the more frequently you talk to someone, the more there is to talk about.

Valerie knew me during the dark years before my face grew big enough to accommodate my nose. She stood by me when I dedicated an entire summer to growing out my bangs. She has patiently listened to the retelling of a 100 first dates and 99 breakups, in real time. She knows when I'm lying or leaving something out. And she'll call me out on it, because, after all, she's not interviewing for my friendship. She's got the job, tenured with full benefits.

Old friends know what you're made of. They know what the end of the world looks like for you, and what it doesn't. When life kicks you in the teeth, you can call your old friend and pour out your heart. "I'll never get over this," you tell her. And she reminds you that that's exactly what you said when you thought Duran Duran was breaking up. And you seem to have gotten over that.

In this sense, old friends put things in perspective. Life has been long, time passes and it will continue to pass. They see patterns in your life and are not afraid to point them out. They also know where you've been wounded, giving you the benefit of their good counsel while saving you the agony of having to retell your life's story.

I am particularly grateful to have Valerie today, at midlife. I highly recommend wading through this tricky time with the same person that you leaned on during adolescence. There's really no difference between the two stages of life: you turn inward, wonder if you look okay and then try to decide where you're going next. I can't tell you how many times I've nodded my head at the TV, thinking, "Wow. That Zoey 101 really knows how I feel."

If life is a sentence, then adolescence and midlife are just commas — there to give us pause and to allow us to move forward with a new subject. Who better to help you figure out who you're going to be for the next 30 years than the person who launched you into the last 30? There's efficiency in not having to explain your parents or your prom date or the essence of what you've always wanted. Your old friend was there when it started.

I am grateful for all of this, but mostly for the laughing. I'm convinced that it affects me on a cellular level. I'm looking forward to old age with Valerie, sitting in rocking chairs with tears streaming down our faces, laughing about when we were in our 40s.

Death, Taxes and Dinner

Much is made of death and taxes. Their unavoidability, the fact that they are always hanging, ominously, just over our shoulders. But death comes about only once in a lifetime, and tax season's just once a year. Dinner, on the other hand, happens every day. Without fail. Every time I start chopping an onion, I think, "Wait. Didn't I just make dinner?" No, I'm afraid that was yesterday. And tomorrow.

The four o'clock panic starts with the slight grumbling of my stomach and ends like a game show. I suddenly remember about dinner — which makes me feel kind of dumb. This isn't my mother-in-law's birthday or Little League signup. It's the main part of my job. When dinner catches me unprepared, I stand in front of my refrigerator and will it to yield a meal. Let's see, I have half a head of broccoli, a handful of mushrooms, two chicken breasts and a hamburger patty. As a general rule, if I have an onion, I can turn anything into dinner.

There are ways around making dinner, including ordering in or buying frozen entrees, things I sometimes do but have been brainwashed to think are worse than tax evasion. Blame my mother. She saw dinner as something more than a plate full of soon-they-won't-be-hungry. It was a ritual of sorts, the preparation of the food was an offering to the time that we would all sit together in festive communion. She would return from a full day of work, somehow with groceries in hand, and happily start cooking. She found it meditative and often said that the most relaxing part of her day was the chopping and sautéing. I guess it takes all kinds.

Sadly, I don't see making dinner as the creative, magical experience that my mom did. This is partially because she was a joy-is-in-the-journey sort, and I am more of a let's-get-stuff-done person. It is also because I am raising kids in an era when they are allowed to have preferences. (I'm not sure whom to blame here, but I'd like to blame somebody.) When I was a kid, there was dinner. And there were kids starving in Africa. Period.

My approach to making dinner is more like a decision-science exercise, where you are trying to get two-dozen shipments of coal to several locations at the highest speed with the lowest cost. The meal itself is a formula: a protein, a starch and a vegetable. And I seek to fill each category and minimize complaints by reviewing the gourmet idiosyncrasies of my picky audience. I stroll through the supermarket aisles mentally sorting through which kid eats green beans but not carrots. Which one won't eat cheese but likes fish. Which one likes turkey meatballs but not turkey burgers (FYI: the ingredients are identical). In the end, we just eat a lot of chicken.

For two magical weeks last winter, I discovered the Crock-Pot, a shortcut that I think my mom would have approved of. It involved the same nurturing, chopping and sautéing but just at a time of day when I still had a little life in me. I loved that Crock-Pot, the feeling of being done with dinner at 9 a.m. It was as if I'd beat the system by paying my whole day forward. But then the inevitable happened — one child rejected the Crock-Pot. All of its meals were too saucy. *Too saucy?* I had a million comebacks, but this is the one kid who never gives me a hard time about brussels sprouts, so I retired that blessed appliance to a high shelf.

Many families have mealtime rules. No phones at the table. No discussing politics, religion or bathroom mishaps. My kids are allowed to talk about anything they want as long as it's not food. If they can't talk about food, it's impossible for them to comment on which food groups are touching. Or lumpy. Or burnt. It's been a small victory to listen to any number of dirty jokes in lieu of "is this a different kind of potato? I liked the other kind of potato …"

Even though I am not the passionate cook that my mom was, I do still love the communion of dinner. The sitting down, the pause. Sometimes dinner is the first time I've sat down all day without a laptop or a steering wheel in front of me. "What happened today?" can be hard to answer because so much happened, so fast. The bad things can be funny in the retelling, which makes the dinner table a place to reframe your experience. "You got knocked down on the playground? A lady yelled at me in the CVS parking lot!" We all laugh. We all learn a few dirty jokes.

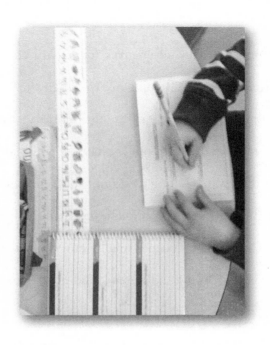

In the Hot Seat

Is there anything more awkward than the parent-teacher conference? It embodies all the stress and apprehension of a performance review with the added discomfort of being perched on a teeny tiny chair. Like most moms, I've squirmed in my fair share of these chairs, waiting to hear the verdict on how my kids are turning out. Any of my kids' teachers can tell you that I become a nervous, babbling, over-explaining version of myself. It's not pretty.

I suspect that my conference anxiety is a throwback to my own elementary school days. My mother was told twice a year, in no uncertain terms, that I was not living up to my potential (really, who is?), and that I talked too much in class (hello, I'm female). As with most things, she had a good sense of humor about it, but I took it to heart. As an adult, I guess I'm still longing for a few words of affirmation from a teacher.

The uninitiated might remark that my son's conference isn't really about me. They'd say the focus should be on him and how he's turning out as a student. Well, I've seen enough slander come home in his backpack to know better. All year, he's been bringing home writing assignments that could have been penned by Kitty Kelley. They are exposés about what really goes on inside our house. He writes about how much time his mom spends "playing Facebook," which episode of "Family Guy" he likes best and how his favorite dinner is frozen taquitos. Woefully absent from his memoirs are the jigsaw puzzle we just slogged through, the fact that I remembered to sign him up for soccer and his up-to-date immunization record. I'm a little defensive about whether his teacher thinks I'm living up to my potential.

These conferences only last 20 minutes, and they're usually running a bit late. I sit outside the classroom, waiting and fidgeting myself into a panic. My kid's doing fine in school, but I dread a line like, "Tell me, is there something going on at home?" What isn't going on at home? We live in a loosely controlled chaos — the love child of overscheduling and sink-or-swim parenting. I want her to tell me that I'm doing a good (enough) job, and that my kid seems to feel confident and loved. I couldn't care less how well he's learning to read. That's her job, not mine.

I sit in my tiny waiting chair, suddenly aware of my hugeness and wondering at my choice of clothing. *Did I make enough of an effort? Or, worse, did I make too much of an effort? Is she going to think I'm a person who spends the whole day blowing her hair dry rather than preparing healthy snacks for the afternoon? Is that why my children are eating frozen taquitos?* I decide to wipe off my lipstick and pull my hair into a ponytail.

When I'm called in, I say hello and shake her hand. I have no idea why I'm being so formal, as I see her every single day at pickup. But here we are alone, with 19 minutes ahead of us to engage in the school district's version of speed dating. Her objective is to tell me how my son is doing in school. My objective is to keep my mouth shut long enough to let her meet her objective. The keeping-my-mouth-shut part proves to be a challenge.

She starts with his progress in reading and nicely comments that she imagines I read to him a lot at home. I could simply nod, but apparently, I need to elaborate. I start to explain how I read much more to my older kids when they were little, but now with all the driving to sports in the evenings, it's hard to fit the reading in. I explain how my middle son plays basketball in two leagues even though he hasn't really grown yet, but that I like to encourage him because I'm short too. I stand to show her just how short I am and assure her that I've turned out fine in spite of it. I am on the verge of confessing to sloth and occasional impure thoughts about Ryan Gosling when I catch her glancing at the clock over my shoulder. I conclude with, "Yes, I read to him" and sit back down. There are now only ten minutes left.

He knows his math facts, whatever that means. I offer, "We do a lot of math at home." Now I'm just plain lying, and she knows it. No one does a lot of math at home. The only math we do sounds like: "If you don't get your shoes on by the time I count to five ..." But I hold her gaze because I desperately want her to forget about the frozen taquitos.

Our conference goes five minutes over, and I find the next nervous parent sitting in the hall in the tiny chair. Behind me, the teacher is scribbling in my son's permanent record, probably something about how his mom talks too much in class.

THINGS COULD BE WORSE

People seem to really like to talk about the good old days. Remember when kids played outside and could shake your hand because they weren't playing Angry Birds? I remember those days too, but here's what I also remember about growing up in the 70's: driving down the freeway, inhaling that first morning puff of secondhand smoke (I still like the smell), and watching my mom swerve a bit because the driver of the car in front of us had chucked the remainder of his McDonald's meal out the window.

This was such a common experience that we didn't even flinch. My mom would just run the windshield wipers a bit and be done with it. I don't know if this was even illegal in 1975.

So now every time I hear someone say how we are all going to hell in a handbasket, that image crosses my mind. I see a strawberry milkshake dripping down the windshield, carrying with it a discarded pickle and maybe an empty ketchup packet. Sure, things aren't perfect today, but the fact that we don't do that anymore shows that we have the potential to improve.

The freeway of my childhood was literally lined on either side with garbage, not just lunch remains but sofa cushions, newspapers and tire irons. Traffic pushed the garbage onto the shoulder the way plows form snowbanks. I honestly never thought anything of it.

Then at some point in elementary school, things changed. It became unpopular to be referred to as a litterbug. I am still not sure if this is an entomological term for an actual bug who chucks his Big Mac wrapper out the window, but being a litterbug was a worse social stigma than having the cooties. Naturally I'd had my cootie shots, but in 1978 there was no inoculation for being a litterbug.

My school had a contest to see who could collect the most pop tops off of the ground around our community. You might recall that sodas used to have pop tops that came all the way off. It was glamorous to pop open your Tab and then drop that little piece of metal into the tall grass, where it would later choke your dog or cut your foot. I collected literally hundreds of pop tops off my school playground and the surrounding few streets, and I wasn't even really trying that hard.

My mind is blown by how far we've come, that this same careless generation has managed to change its habits. The early days of recycling required so much personal retraining that I wondered if it would ever catch on. *You mean I am going to have to separate my garbage? Like, touch it? Are you kidding?* But now we design our kitchens around the task, and the separating is unconscious. My kids would sooner eat cauliflower than put a plastic bottle in the regular garbage.

Plastic bags are illegal in my town. You can't even buy a plastic bag with a permit and a four-day waiting period, that's how illegal they are. Carrying reusable bags is a major behavioral change, and we embraced it because it involved a bit of social pressure. If I forget my bags and have to take the paper ones offered by the store, I am awash with the childhood stigma of being a litterbug. We have even repurposed the phrase "walk of shame" to describe the trip through the parking lot carrying these wasteful bags.

I wonder if my kids can even fathom the madness of my childhood. Their generation is miles ahead of us and my hope is that they will keep us out of that quickly descending handbasket. They learn songs at school about the subtleties of recycling different types of paper: "If it's grey, throw it away; if it's brown, pass it down." That really beats "If you're done with your fries, just chuck them out the window." Which doesn't even rhyme. I think there's hope for us yet.

Warning: It's Christmas and Mom Might Snap

One of my favorite holiday traditions is watching stuff I've seen a hundred times and sobbing in front of my television. By the time Harry Bailey says, "To my big brother George, the richest man in town," I'm pretty much a mess. Among these odes to the season, my very favorite happens to be a holiday episode of "Family Guy." It's sacrilege to even mention it in the same paragraph as "It's a Wonderful Life," but it leaves me crying with laughter, which I tend to prefer.

The beauty of this episode is that it reveals one of the purest truths of the Christmas season, that every mom you see is filled with both the warm spirit of the holiday and the potential to snap at any moment.

To summarize: The episode begins with Lois, loving mother, admiring the star atop the tree in the town square. She comments on the miracle of the season, the importance of family and love for all mankind. Her children are greedy and ungrateful, and her bumbling husband accidentally gives all of her family's Christmas gifts away. Later her tree catches fire, as does the living room and the turkey. No problem. At least they all have each other and the promise of the joy of the season.

Then Lois runs out of paper towels. It's just paper towels, not a big thing when you consider what's already happened. But she snaps in a manner completely out of proportion to the situation, jumps through the kitchen window and runs down the street screaming.

It's a lot of pressure to be the mom at Christmas. It's like being the director, producer, set designer and playwright for a month-long show. It's more than just the gifts and decorations. It's the mom's job to create the magic. We strive to create an atmosphere of warmth and excitement that will stay with our kids forever, as if the quality of their Christmas memories is going on our permanent record. It's a 25-day photo op, and the stakes are high.

As the first window of the Advent calendar opens, the memory making begins. Christmas looks like twinkly lights, sounds like Bing Crosby and smells like butter and sugar cooking at 375 degrees. We resurrect old family recipes that were penned, presumably, back when there were 58 hours in a day. We agree to attend a cookie party without reading the fine print – "please bring seven dozen cookies." *What?!* That's usually the first snap of the season.

But we regroup and try to look chipper. We wear too-bright red sweaters and dress our already frumpy cars in antlers. The car antlers, to me, are the definitive sign that the driver is just two dozen cookies away from a straight jacket. Look, they scream, I've run out of things to decorate!

In a sense, December is the Super Bowl of being a mom. We do all of the above things, plus we still have to do our regular jobs. Life doesn't stop for the production of Christmas. Stuff still breaks during the holidays, socks still need to be matched, kids still need stitches. In short, just because I'm making a special roast on the 25th doesn't mean my family isn't hungry on every one of the 24 days before that.

The years that I've snapped, it's been about something as trivial as paper towels. I'm prepared for the tree to burn down. And, sure, I'll get the flu. 99 percent guaranteed. But it's the tiny unexpected things that bring me to a running-out-of-paper-towels moment. Once (okay, yesterday) I snapped when I realized that the holiday cards I'd ordered came with envelope liners that needed to be individually inserted into the envelopes by me. Seems like no big deal, right? It nearly took me down.

I've worried about Santa. Would he ever snap? All that hot cocoa and jolly laughter. Something's bound to give. Will there ever come a time when one too many requests for a Princess Anna sleeping bag sends him over the edge? See, I think not. Santa's advantage is that he only has to do the one thing. I've watched a lot of Christmas movies, and I've never seen him throw in a load of laundry or file an amendment to his tax return. In fact he's pretty well staffed, and it seems like kind of a seamless operation. Our kids tell him exactly what they want, and the elves make all the stuff. Santa seems to be the frontman, primarily in charge of PR and delivery. From what I can tell, the guy only works like two days a year.

If you look closely at Mrs. Claus, you will see she's not quite so rosy. You know she's had it with remembering the Elf on the Shelf and looking for the Scotch tape. I'm sure she'd agree that, in the end, it's all worth it, that there's not one aspect of Christmas we'd agree to give up. It really is a magic time. But I'm definitely stocking up on paper towels this year.

Mail Fraud

My mailbox is filling up with holiday cards. It's one of my very favorite parts of the season. These ink-on-paper cards give me all the voyeuristic joys of Facebook, but with photos that you can actually touch. They are magical, all those smiling faces and catchy holiday wishes — windows into the lives of the families who sent them.

And then there's my family's holiday card: the big fat lie that I distribute annually through the mail.

My philosophy has always been that there's no room in the holiday card for reality. Every year I produce this costly document, to be preserved for the ages, as a snapshot in the year of my family. And it's propaganda like you wouldn't believe. The photo is always taken outside in some beautiful venue that, to the untrained eye, might be an exotic vacation spot or even a summer home. The one I sent last year with all the fall foliage could have been the day we went apple picking. Two things you should know: We're an extremely indoorsy family, and we have never been apple picking. Ever. We don't even eat much fruit.

The second step in this farce is costume design. My kids frolic in co-ordinating sweaters in holiday colors and clean, pressed pants. I look back and wonder: Who are these children? My kids don't wear sweaters. Or clean pants. The receiver of this card marvels at the casual elegance of my children and the implied beauty of my life. I must have a lot of staff and probably a couple of horses.

The photo that makes the cut always features my kids laughing in delight. You know, the way kids generally sit in a neat row and laugh at the sheer pleasure of being together and having their photo taken in uncomfortable clothing. They are often looking at each other as if the pure goodness and comedic genius of their brothers will sustain Christmas joy the whole year through. The truth is they're laughing at me. Not with me — at me. I've just taken 50 photos and have screamed, "You sit there and look happy or ELSE!" They find this hilarious.

This year a little reality snuck back into my card. I don't know how it happened. Time and patience being as scarce as they are, I just picked a day when everyone's hair was reasonably clean and no one had a black eye. I skipped the costume design in favor of the Under Armor couture that they were already wearing and made them sit in front of our front door. Reality, you ask? How often do you happen upon three kids squeezed uncomfortably together in front of their front door? I know, it's a stretch, but it actually was where we vacationed this year. I snapped a few photos with my phone until I threw a tantrum large enough to make them smile.

Next year I'm considering giving up the game altogether and just snapping the three of them in the basement in their pajamas, Xbox controllers in hand, with the hint of Cheetos dust coloring their lips. The beauty of my family lives in those messy moments. But who really wants to see that?

THE PLAYDATE PYRAMID SCHEME

Had any good playdates lately? Me neither. Well, except for the one that was at the other kid's house. That one was pretty painless. I arrived a few minutes late to pick up my kindergartener, invigorated by all that I'd accomplished with the extra two hours to myself. The other mom greeted me at the door before I had made it all the way down the walkway, unconsciously looking at her watch. She had a smile on her face but had developed a slight facial tic that I hadn't noticed before. She had my son's shoes and backpack right by the door to expedite our departure and seemed to visibly relax as we headed to the car. She'd served her time.

Let's face it — playdates are brutal. And they stay brutal until the kids start calling them something else. By the time my kids say, "Can Ryan come over to hang out?" the pain of the playdate is over. Kids that come over to hang out are old enough to entertain themselves and solve their own conflicts. Since hangouts are scheduled by kids, and not parents, the kids have selected each other based on compatibility. The success of a hangout doesn't generally hinge on magic markers, costume changes or me posing as a mummy while they wrap me in toilet paper.

The playdate set, which I will define loosely as ages three to eight, is all about satisfying immediate needs and really not at all about decorum. They open up my refrigerator and pull out the gallon of orange juice, declaring, "I need a cup." They take a bite of their lunch and say they're full and then ask for a snack, almost all in one breath. If you tell them you don't have any snacks, they go into your pantry to prove you're a liar: "You've got cookies!" If the play date starts to get a little boring, they come right out and call it: "Your house is boring." Little kids have no filter.

And then there's always the kid who needs a little more help in the bathroom than I'm entirely comfortable giving. He finds nothing awkward about the situation and seems to find it strange that I do. I've already said too much.

The most exhausting thing about playdates with little ones is that you really cannot take your eyes off them, even for a second. It seems to be some sort of rite of passage for every child under the age of six to come into my home and find the heaviest toy possible and drop it from the highest point on my staircase onto my (now dented) floors. Worse, I once caught a five-year-old out on the railing of a second-floor balcony attempting a pretty impressive balance beam performance. I pulled him to safety and tried to explain how dangerous that was. His eyes told me that if he knew the phrase "buzzkill," he would have used it.

So, if the playdate is going to last two hours, you have to get off the phone, shut down the computer and be vigilant. But it's totally worth it because you will have accomplished two things:

1. You have exposed your small child to an experiment in socializing, compromising and sharing (yawn).

2. You have just bought yourself two hours of free time when that other kid's mom reciprocates. It's like a modern-day barter system, a co-op parenting strategy.

I've recently taken things up a notch. Please try to follow my math, as I am about to blow your mind. Because I know that I am going to be watching over two children for two hours in order to purchase two hours of free time, why not watch over three children for two hours to purchase four hours of free time? This is identical in concept to syndicating a column: you work once and get paid multiple times. About halfway through kindergarten, I broke through to another dimension. I started inviting four boys for a playdate at the same time. The math: I supervise five boys for two mind-bending hours to purchase eight hours of free time. The Nobel Prize people should be calling any day now.

The playdates have gotten easier as kindergarten has gone along, just as they did with my older sons and their friends. The kids get to be more relaxed with each other, and they've figured out what works and what doesn't. This time around, I take none of it personally, because I know it'll get better. The big kids who come to hang out at my house now clear their own plates and thank me six times for every meal. They like my pork chops and inquire about my choice of seasoning. These are the same kids who told me my sandwiches tasted yucky years ago.

A Californian in Winter

No matter how long we're away and how pale we become, there are subtle ways to spot a Californian. We say "freeway" instead of "highway," we wait "in line" rather than "on line." Pop quiz: do you happen to know the date of the Academy Awards this year? Yes? Then you're a Californian. An even easier way to spot a Californian is to expose us to a little weather. We missed the childhood of snowmen and mittens. If we look a little baffled, it's because we were not bred for this stuff.

There is so much to know about snow. My Canadian husband throws around terms like "heavy snow" and "wet snow," and my half-Canadian kids know which kind is good for snowmen. Apparently snow itself is not the enemy, unless it brings wind and becomes a blizzard that will knock out your power lines. Then snow's a big deal.

When the temperature warms a few degrees above freezing, I foolishly think things are getting better. But those in the know brace themselves for the mini-melt and subsequent refreeze that will turn my driveway into an ice rink. My kids understand this process the way I grew up understanding why you turn your beach towel with the movement of the sun to avoid an imbalanced suntan. (This information has not proved to be valuable during the past few months.)

I've learned that ice is worse than snow like the stomach flu is worse than a two-hour massage. There's something called "ice rain," which can be explained to Californians in this way: it's like if you opened your poolside ice maker and just started chucking the cubes around. But not as fun. It turns out ice can form in your pipes, freezing them until they burst. Oddly, the resulting flood comes out in liquid form rather than in cubes. Why isn't it frozen? People from the Northeast can explain this. They're practically scientists.

Worse than regular ice is the sinister black ice, which is sneaky and invisible and so deadly that roads and schools shut down in fear. Black ice broke my babysitter's wrist, and she's got six to ten more weeks in a cast. I've recently learned the term "ice dam," which is a catastrophe that elicits empathetic nods from people around here. It's pretty much the worst thing that can happen to you, and there's no cure for it. I think of an ice dam as the herpes of winter.

Explaining all of this to my friends and family in Los Angeles is a bit like explaining the plot of Star Wars to George Washington. It's a different world with different rules and constraints, and, unless you've cruised in the Millennium Falcon, you can't understand what it's like. "Why are your kids home from school again? What do you mean Tom's car is 'frozen-in'"? It's at times like this that I feel like California is light years away.

I've seen things from their side. I happened to be stranded in Los Angeles during Hurricane Sandy. And I hear it was a real whopper! I'd be sitting poolside, listening to my husband's voice on the phone, "It's 30 degrees in our house, a tree fell on our deck ..." I'd think: *That sounds terrible ... wait, didn't I ask for salt on this margarita?* In defense of Californians, it's incongruous to try to wrap your head around the freezing, wet horror when you smell like sunscreen. It almost sounded like they were making it up.

I am slowly learning my way around shoveling, deicing and salting. I know the joy that comes from seeing the dry blacktop on my driveway. But here's another phrase I never knew growing up: "green shoots." The green shoots that poke out of the ground on the first warmish day of spring are the visual embodiment of hope. The exhilaration that they bring to our still-bundled selves is like a double paddle of the defibrillator, a small payback for winter. It's a rhythm that mimics life, the dark days followed by the magnolia blossoms. And it's almost worth it. Almost.

CRACKING THE DRESS CODE

A few weeks ago, I was invited to a dinner party and was told in plain English to wear a dress. Honestly, I was just as happy to have been told what to wear as I was to be going to a party. A dress! What could be easier? But when I arrived at the party, I found out that I was in the wrong dress. It was too casual by several standard deviations, and I spent the evening with that middle-school feeling that I didn't quite fit in. The direction I needed was "A cocktail dress, your best one."

I dream of a world where invitations come with visual aids, maybe a hologram or a little cartoon of exactly what the hostess is going to be wearing. Instead I find that we have a coded language of baffling phrases that is meant to guide us on the path to appropriateness. Navigating a party invitation can be like cracking "The Da Vinci Code."

Here's one phrase I don't find helpful: Festive Casual Attire. What does that even mean? Like my black exercise pants and a sparkly top? My pajamas with a sombrero and some maracas? Same goes for City Chic. I rifle through my frumpy suburban closet for black things with grommets. I dab tobacco behind my ears and search the internet to see what Nicole Richie's wearing. She too, apparently, is out of date.

(Dress to Impress is another puzzler that tells me nothing but the fact that I'm about to disappoint my hostess.)

Black Tie, I love. I have two things in two sizes. One bag goes with both, and I'm ready to go. Business Attire, on the other hand, bugs me on both a practical and philosophical level. There was a day when this was the easiest of all. I'd show up in whatever suit I'd been wearing all day and fit right in. Now it just makes me a little defensive about my "business." What if you're a welder or a stripper or a writer? I'm surprised there hasn't been more outrage on this topic, like when the peach crayon used to be called "flesh." Business Attire should really read: "Dress like a member of Congress." Though, to be honest, if I put on one of my old suits it would be more like: dress like a member of the cast of Dynasty.

Occasionally, the hostess won't give you a dress code, but she will give you clues that will lead only the cleverest few of her guests to the right ensemble. Take Lawn Party, for example. I've learned this one the hard way. The first time I saw this cryptic phrase, I took it to mean that I'd need a sweater. Incorrect! I can still recall the exact moment when my spiked heels started sinking into the grass, tilting me dangerously backward. Lawn Party, it turns out, means "Wear flat or wedged shoes. And bug spray." Would that have been so hard to say? The party was divided between the cryptologists and those whose heels were stuck in the lawn like golf tees.

It's all very subtle and probably a little bit graceful. Nobody wants to come across as bossing around her guests. But would it ruin the mystery to say: "Come for summer cocktails! Everyone's going to be in white pants and a colorful top?" Or, better: "Come for dinner. Wear your black dress. Not the one with the lace around the neck, that's going to make you look like you're trying too hard, but it's okay to wear your new super-high shoes because we'll mostly be sitting." I'd be so grateful.

LOST AND FOUND

It usually starts with "Mooooom …" Though it sometimes starts with "Hoooooooney …" I hear it more in my lower back than in my ears, because I know this plea for help often leads to a trip down the rabbit hole. It's the moment that some member of my family cannot immediately find the item that he's looking for. He's looked in the one spot he thought it would be and didn't see it. We are moments away from pure madness.

This doesn't happen with easily replaceable things, like the glass of water he was just drinking or a pair of white socks. It's the uniform for the game that's starting in an hour or the only set of keys to the car. The item is critical, the stakes are high and the clock is ticking.

I stay very calm. At first. I go back to the place where it was supposed to be and relook, mainly because this is not my first rodeo. I look under things. I sometimes wonder if my kids missed that peek-a-boo phase of development where you learn the concept of object permanence. Just because your phone's under a baseball hat doesn't mean it's not there.

Once I've exhausted the two most likely places the item might be, we collectively start to panic. I try not to get sucked in, but panic truly is contagious. And when this happens, a fog falls over all of us, and we become visually impaired. We have opened our eyes to the fact that this thing could be gone forever, and from then on we cannot see anything but the absence of the object. We walk in and out of rooms. We paw through the laundry basket. It's just not there. We look again.

The fog leads to the flashbacks, and that's when the door to the rabbit hole opens. We descend single file. The owner of the lost item speculates that he had the item with him last week and thinks he remembers putting it down on the bleachers. But he thinks he had it again at Will's house on Friday. Or maybe it was in his backpack, which he remembers leaving open and unattended for an hour at that scrimmage.

Obviously, it's been stolen. This is a favorite theory in my family. With all the things in my house that have disappeared via theft, it's weird that all my jewelry's still here. And the TV. It's just muddy cleats and a favorite pair of blue exercise shorts that they're after. Criminals are a mysterious breed.

Now that we are all the way down the rabbit hole, we are no longer looking in the house. I am on the phone with neighboring school districts asking them to check their lost-and-founds. Sure, I'll hold. Someone drives to the field to check the bleachers. We've left three voicemails for Will's mom. We are a frenzy of motion and loud voices and circular arguments. We stop short of calling the police.

The last time this happened (Tuesday), it got so bad that my survival skills kicked in. I had the presence of mind to try to make my way back to the surface. I said to the supremely panicked person, "I will find this, but I need to get your energy out of this house." Oddly, he knew exactly what I meant. See, this wasn't his first rodeo either. He was out of the house for five minutes before I regained my sight and ten minutes before I found that thing. It was in the laundry basket that we'd been through three times.

EXTREME MAKEOVER: GROCERY ADDITION

Remember how you felt that time you went to the office Christmas party and met the attractive young woman that just started working with your husband? And remember how you noticed for the first time that your cocktail dress, circa 1998, was somehow too long, too short and too snug all at once? The very next day you barreled into the plastic surgeon's office and demanded "the works." We've all been there. I'm pretty sure that's how my old, reliable Stop & Shop feels now that the new Whole Foods is opening up right down the street.

You can feel the panic the instant you walk in there. Stop & Shop is in the midst of the fight of its life, and it's opted for an extreme makeover. With the facelift nearly complete, I have to admit I kind of miss the old version. The pre-op store did a pretty good job selling grocery staples and good-enough produce. It was just the basics, everything you needed. No surprises. I knew my way around without really even paying attention. It's possible that I've heard my husband describe me in the exact same way.

You can't blame them for panicking. How are they supposed to sell people a package of Perdue chicken when a mile away you can get certified humanely raised chicken? Once I have options, I'll probably never eat a tortured chicken again. I'm starting to wonder if the energy of that poor chicken, blindfolded and marched to his death, has been keeping me down. How is Stop & Shop supposed to compete with happy chickens and the promise of a better life?

I'm trying to stay loyal to my saggy old market, even as it squeezes itself into a younger woman's jeans. I nod cheerfully at the new cheese section, which houses the exact same cheeses as before, but is arranged vertically rather than horizontally. I overlook the fact that the lettuces are now sense-lessly located in three separate spots. I want to make this work.

And I'm not alone. The newly revamped store is packed with dazed but loyal customers, pushing empty carts through the now slightly wider but completely mixed-up aisles. The nip and tuck has resulted in something unnatural, and the new (dis)order is baffling. We mumble as we try to reorient ourselves: "Why is there bleach next to the corn chips?" "Where'd the bread go?"

Well, if you really want to know, I'll tell you where the bread went. While the bread used to be in the center of the market, a location suitable for the staff of life, it is now pushed to the left-hand corner. It's a corner that feels like a shameful place, where one might keep any other dark, dirty secret. For emphasis, someone seems to have shot out the corner lights, making gluten fiends feel like they're in the midst of a back-alley transac-tion as they snatch their Wonder Bread and scurry away.

On the opposite side of the store is a brightly lit oasis. It includes two aisles labeled "Natural Foods," which begs the question: what kind of food is in the rest of the store? (This is sort of like when you get your eyes done and then you're suddenly aware that your neck looks like a turkey's wattle.) In these natural aisles, you can feel like you're actually in Whole Foods, surrounded by organic almond butter, chia seeds and six kinds of farro. This area abuts the new natural meat section where you can buy organic chicken, though the butcher makes no claims about how they were treated.

By the time the scars heal on this nip and tuck, we'll be used to the new store. We'll start to appreciate the effort they've made and will forgive them for the confusion. But please, dear Stop & Shop, don't fret — we're never going to leave you. Don't ever underestimate our dependence on routine. And, as alluring as pampered chickens can seem, we still need a place to buy Bisquick, Skippy and Eggos. You can't get that stuff at Whole Foods.

The Agony (and Zen) of Little League

"How much longer does this go?" I ask the parent next to me. "It's only the first inning," she responds. *What?!* I have this conversation several times a week during the start of baseball season. How could my buns have gone numb against these metal bleachers in only one inning? I check my watch. I check my phone. I wonder why no one else looks like they're trapped in an elevator. I'm sure my hair's grown an inch since this game started.

A little kids' baseball game can start to feel like a hostage situation. The fact that it might last for three hours could be the reason that it's called America's pastime. By the bottom of the third, I'm pretty much thinking it's past time. I spend the first few games of the season resisting baseball in this way, mentally willing that kid in center field to catch just one fly ball to move things along.

For me, baseball is like yoga. From the expressions of concentration on the faces around me, I have the sense that something very important is happening, yet I see almost nothing happening at all. I get fidgety and start making mental lists. Everyone else seems to have come seeking this slower pace, and I'm baffled by their collective tranquility.

You can probably tell that I need baseball and yoga more than anyone. I tend to approach a Saturday with a list and move through the events on that list as quickly as possible to obtain that fleeting sense of accomplishment that comes with having gotten in bed at night with a list all checked off. I'm a bit hooked on getting stuff done, which is probably why I like basketball. In at noon, out at one o'clock. On to the next thing. Watching a red-faced child stumble off of a basketball court gives me the sense that much has been achieved in an economical amount of time.

Yoga is avoidable, but baseball keeps dragging me back in year after year. And each season, around the third game, I surrender to the fact that there's just no rushing in baseball. I start bringing my own chair. I start bringing my own drinks. I stop planning things for the afternoon. I notice the newly familiar faces around me, and I edge my way into their conversations. All lined up, watching I'm-not-sure-what, the conversation is easy and is seldom about baseball. I start to hate it less.

I start noticing that people bring their parents, and I start noticing how much I want to talk to people's parents. I scoot my folding chair closer to the older generation, and soon I start to kind of like baseball. I ask them questions, they tell me stories. Long stories. They're not the sort of stories you can fit into a Facebook post or a tweet. In fact, older people don't feel at all compelled to make a long story short. We're at a baseball game, after all. We have all the time in the world.

When a seventy-five-year-old man meets you for the first time, he immediately recognizes you as a new set of ears. He starts in with some well-seasoned small talk, and then he brings out his best stuff: The time he met Jimmy Carter, the time he dated his wife's sister and realized he had the wrong girl, the distance he walked to caddy as a kid and the lessons he learned eavesdropping on golfers. My father-in-law has a story about the time his four-year-old brother wandered off to the movie house during the war. I've heard it a dozen times, and I can't do it justice. In a lifetime, a person accumulates maybe ten great stories. A baseball game is almost long enough to share five of them.

Meanwhile, someone kicks up some dust, someone finally makes contact with the ball and little children are running the bases, over and over. My heart rate is down, and my pulse has slowed to the rhythm of the game. People around us start to pack up their coolers, but the last story's not quite over. We make no move to leave. I'm not sure what the big hurry was anyway.

THE 70S REALLY SCREWED ME UP

Everyone says the media's ruining our kids. It gives them a warped sense of how people should look, how people behave and what the real world's going to be like when they get there. We like to blame the media like it's new, like there's been a management change on Madison Avenue, and the new guys no longer know how to grow young people into wholesome, perfect adults like us. The truth is that the television commercials that were responsible for forming my worldview in the 1970s painted such a wacky image of what being a woman was going to be like that I approached adulthood with some trepidation.

According to the television of my childhood, when I became a wife and mother, the one thing I'd want above all things would be to keep 'em home for breakfast. I'd stop at nothing to keep my kids from getting on that bus or my husband from escaping with his briefcase. I'd be desperate to keep them home — desperate enough to feed them commercially prepared cake at eight in the morning. Boy, was I duped. As a wife and mother, I fail to see any circumstances short of a nuclear disaster that would make me want to delay the blessed morning departure of my family. I now wonder what that woman was so afraid of, what was going to be so bad about being home alone. Truly, the only thing that delights me more than seeing those smiling faces return at the end of the day is knowing that they are going to leave again in the morning.

I also learned that grown women have fetishes for sneaking around the supermarket in hopes of squeezing the toilet paper without the store manager seeing. They actually can't bear to pass toilet paper without fondling it, and will go to any length to cop a feel. What mad world was I being prepared for? I have (almost) never had any such urge.

Alternatively, my TV told me, I could grow up to be a woman who chose to bring home the bacon. I would then proceed to fry it up in a pan and then do some unnamed thing involving perfume that would never, ever let my husband forget he was a man. I imagine my actual grown self returning from work and wrestling the spatula away from my husband, insisting that I be the one to prepare dinner. In my adult reality, I don't bring home the bacon, and I'm sort of tired of cooking dinner. Is there a perfume for that?

I don't know what ever happened to Yuban coffee, but these commercials particularly freaked me out. They led me to believe that whatever my career path, I would eventually become my husband's mother. If someone offered him (gasp!) a second cup of coffee, I was to immediately jump in and admonish the hostess: "Jim never has a second cup at home." Further, should he actually want that second cup of coffee, I was to be personally offended because I was going to grow up to be a person who was competitive about coffee. Not only do I not feel responsible for how much coffee my husband drinks, if I'm going to someone's house in the evening, it's not to drink coffee.

You can see why I was a little overwhelmed by all that womanhood had to offer me — the job, the chores, the neuroses. The lady at the nail salon was going to trick me into soaking my hands in dishwashing liquid. All this was going to be some sort of an improvement because, after all, we'd come

a long way, baby.

Now when I watch TV, I think: so what if my kids grow up thinking

that birth control is something to sing about while performing synchro-

nized swimming routines? Calgon, take me away.

How I Became Irish

During the first 25 years of my life, I frequently had this conversation: "What's your last name?" "It's Schwedes." "What?" "It's Schwedes, pronounced Shway-dis, and spelled like Schweppes, the tonic water, but you've got to drop one "p" and then flip the other one upside down."

As you can imagine, whomever I was talking to would lose interest early on. It's a German name and one that I don't really relate to. Aren't the

Germans supposed to be precise and tidy and smart about their finances? There's no way I'm more than a tiny bit German.

When a man named Monaghan proposed to me, you'd better believe I said yes in a hurry. I never spell it. No one even asks me to. I don't care if the silent "g" makes it in there or not. Pronounce it Moynahan if you want, I couldn't care less. With a quick "I do," I became Irish and easy to deal with, like I always should have been. I know a few things about beer and potatoes. And I don't really tan. It didn't take long before I had children with names like leprechauns, and I started decorating my house for St. Patrick's Day. My poor Spanish grandmother (Mom's side) hardly recognizes me as the matriarch of this family.

So with all this enthusiasm for my new heritage, you'd think I would have legally changed my name. I actually meant to. I'm generally an all-in sort of person, particularly where my family is concerned. Changing your name can be a touchy topic, particularly among women who have established themselves in a career. They feel torn between giving up their hard-earned reputation and making things confusing.

I had neither of these concerns. I wasn't exactly a world-renowned anything before I was married. In fact I dreamed of all the things I could accomplish if I didn't have to spend the day spelling my name to people. But there was something about giving up my quirky tonic-water name that didn't sit right with me. It might be I didn't feel like dealing with the paperwork, or maybe that deep down I thought it was sort of unnecessary and off balance. My husband wasn't changing his name, so was this marriage thing really more of a transaction than a union? And if I changed my name for good, where would that younger self be?

My solution was to keep that younger self and give her all of the hardworking German stuff to deal with. Miss Schwedes is listed on a marriage certificate, three birth certificates, a tax return and a mortgage. She's got a lot of problems. But as consolation she's virtually un-Googleable, so if she was mean to you in middle school (sorry!), and you feel like getting a little revenge, you won't find her. She's shuffled off her German coil and is hanging out at the pub.

I've given all the fun stuff to the Irish lass. She's decidedly more laid back, has lots of friends and does a job she really likes. She has no debt. She doesn't even have a medical history, so I imagine she's in pretty good health. I believe this is what they call the luck of the Irish.

Astronauts

It's funny when your kids start driving and noticing how frequently the adults around them don't obey the traffic laws. "Look, Mom, that guy didn't signal. Look, Mom, that lady ran the stop sign." Don't worry, I filled them in. I simply explained to my kids that these people are a bunch of astronauts (pronounced *ass*-tro-nauts).

Or, at least, I assume they're astronauts, because our earthly laws don't seem to interest them. It's our job to look the other way as they zoom through life at warp speed, double-parking if they have to stop for Tang.

Astronauts are highly trained people, with billions of dollars of research and equipment riding on their full concentration and success. Do you think they really have the mental energy to tell the driver behind them that they plan to turn left? Of course not, they're headed to infinity and beyond! And if that happens to be to the left, then the civilians behind them can enjoy the surprise.

When the space shuttle is scheduled to go, it's scheduled to go. NASA's not going to wait just because its lead astronaut had to drive 20 mph in a school zone. When you see her zipping by at 8:30 a.m. like she's in a high-speed chase, just remember what's really at stake. Same goes for the guy who's roaring past you on the shoulder of the highway. It's a little known fact that the highway shoulder was the brainchild of the space program. You can't expect someone who moves through space at 17,500 mph to sit in traffic.

Ditto for idling. The extra time it takes to turn off the ignition and then back on again could unravel a carefully prepared mission. Not to mention the indignity of being slightly too hot or slightly too cold. (Though you'd think the space suit would adjust for that. Hmm.)

Speaking of that cumbersome space suit, when I happen upon a car parked in not one, but two parking spots, I laugh to myself, *Ah! We have an astronaut in our midst.* A person in a huge spacesuit and helmet cannot be expected to squeeze out of her car with another one crammed right next to her. She pulls in right down the dividing line, so she doesn't smudge her nice white suit on your dirty Suburban. If astronauts need anything, it's space.

In a pinch, astronauts will ride the train. They show up around rush hour, and we need to be mindful of the precious cargo they cart around. Those might look like normal handbags and briefcases taking up the coveted seat next to them, but they likely contain moon rocks or Martian mud or the keys to the space station. You can't expect somebody to just put that stuff in their lap. I want to remind the tired commuters that the sacrifice that they are making by standing up all the way home is in the name of science. It may feel like a small cramp in your left leg, but really it's a giant leap for mankind.

Remember that astronauts need to be in constant contact with ground control, so if they are first in line at a traffic light and that light turns green, and they don't go anywhere, just be cool about it. When that text goes through, and they're good and ready, we'll have liftoff.

A Case for Polygamy

I'm starting to really rethink this whole monogamy thing. No, I haven't met anyone, but in the aftermath of a big power outage, I found myself in possession of sister wives. And I'm not sure I'm willing to go back to the way things were.

I live in a very male household. The only pink item in our house is a breast cancer awareness pepper grinder. We do not have a single Barbie doll or set of fairy wings. No one notices my clothing or the slightly lighter tint of my hair. If we're talking, it's about the Knicks, the Spurs, the Giants or the Steelers. Not one of us knows how to apply mascara properly.

So when my power went out and then was miraculously restored on the ninth day, I had two friends come stay at my house with their families. In the first few hours, we circled the island in my kitchen, not knowing who the top hen was or where we all stood in the pecking order. We didn't want to step on each other's toes or be bossy about how things got done. It was my coop after all, and I think they were waiting to see how I operated.

Then one of the sister wives mentioned that she had a chicken dish she liked to make and asked if we would be interested in having that for dinner. *Gasp! Sigh! Swoon!* That was pretty much it for me. I wouldn't have cared if she was scolding my children or flirting with my husband. The woman came up with something to make for dinner. And then (wait for it ...) she left for the supermarket to get the ingredients.

At three o'clock the normal bedlam kicked in, times three. The kids were home, excited to see their new siblings and scurried off to play. The sister wives and I tag-teamed on laundry, took turns driving kids to sporting events and caught up in a slow, meandering way that I didn't know how much I missed.

I grew up in a household of women. For much of my childhood it was my mom, my sister and me. We did a lot of talking. We could rehash a dinner party, a sideways glance or the neckline of a dress for hours. Women talk about an event and how they felt about it. And then we like to go back and describe how our feelings about said event have evolved over time. It's what we think of as conversation, and this may be why men avoid conversation with women with such determination.

In a house full of boys, there isn't this sense of rehashing, or just conversation for its own sake. Boys use words to convey information or to make requests. "I'm hungry" or "Can you drive me to Ryan's?" are staples. My boys don't start conversations with, "You know what I was thinking about today?" or "Do you think my hair would look better if ..." It's baffling.

The sister wives and I drank tea until teatime turned into cocktail hour. We made dinner. We fed the children and the menfolk as they rolled in, one by one. We wondered to each other which of the husbands we'd choose to keep if we really were to become sister wives. There was a pretty good case for keeping each of them. And we laid out their worst flaws for comparison: The first husband makes too many lists. The second one doesn't know where anything is, and the third one works from home. The third guy didn't stand a chance.

On a Tuesday, one of them got her power back, and the other got her's back soon after. Life got back to normal, and the testosterone imbalance was restored. I'm hoping they'll come back, even when they don't have to, with tea and wine and suggestions about what to make for dinner.

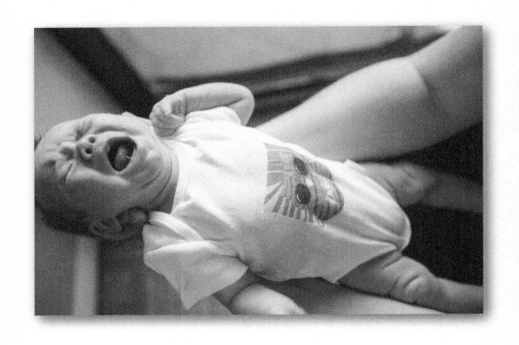

An Open Letter to That Lady
With the Screaming Baby

I'm watching you walk back and forth with that baby in your arms. You wear a path like a dog on a chain. You just laughed at the joke someone in your party told, but you laughed too late, and I can tell you didn't get it. I'm guessing you haven't slept more than twelve hours in the past six weeks. It's all I can do not to run over to you and shower you with my hard-earned wisdom, but I control myself because I remember what it was like to be a new mom.

When I was a new mom, there seemed to be no boundary between strangers and me. They swarmed me with advice and admonishments. As a rule, their comments made me feel like I was a danger to my child.

One day a woman stopped me on the street to declare, not say, but declare as if it were an irrefutable fact of the universe, "That baby is going to die of suffocation in that sweater." I nearly cried. Did she have any idea how long it took the two of us to get out of the house that morning? Did she not know that just the day before another well-meaning woman had told me my sweaterless child was going to freeze to death? To death!

So I don't approach you, New Mom. I'd rather leave you alone and just hope that you pick up this article during a midnight feeding. I want you to know that you have not been Punk'd. This moment that you find yourself in with this six-week-old baby is not what motherhood is going to be. Swaying from side to side, trying to follow an adult conversation about things you no longer feel a part of is not the culmination of that big wedding and festive baby shower. This is just a moment.

I also want you to know that your baby has colic. People might be telling you he's a little fussy or that he takes after his cranky Uncle Al. Or they wonder if you eat too much dairy while nursing, or not enough. They'll tell you he's screaming because you don't let him sleep on his stomach or because you had an epidural during delivery. You're secretly afraid that he's defective in some way. I tell you it's colic, and I'm guessing you have another six weeks left. After consulting many doctors, I have determined that colic is loosely defined as: there's nothing at all wrong with you or your baby, but he's gonna scream for the longest three months of your life.

And if there was an audio component to that definition, it would surely be the sound of your baby crying. Your baby's cry is not a regular "I'm hungry" or "I'm tired" or "You just scraped my back with your watch" cry. It's a screech as loud, jarring and rhythmic as a car alarm. Except car alarms have an auto shut-off function that kicks in after ten minutes. This scream evokes sympathy so deep in me that I want to run over to you and cover your ears.

You just caught my eye. You think I'm staring at you because of the screaming baby. I want you to know that the screaming doesn't bother me a bit. It's not my car alarm. What bothers me is that I have seen you try to sit down to eat three times tonight. And every time you try to pass that baby off to a friend and make contact with the picnic bench, the impact activates the car alarm. That baby does not want you to eat or sit. I want you to know that you are going to sustain your own life by snacking while swaying and standing for another two months. And then it'll be okay.

When the women gather and tell you how beautiful your baby is, how lucky you are and how this is the happiest, most precious time of your life, I want you to know they are out of their minds. They have grown children who are drinking and dating and talking back. They don't remember what it was like to sleep for only 90 minutes at a time and to have scabby nipples. You are not the first person to think maybe this whole motherhood thing wasn't such a good idea. You are not the first person to fantasize about maybe being hospitalized with some minor ailment for three days so that you can sleep.

You probably have a few friends who've just had babies too. And you probably have a friend whose baby slept through the night the first day he came home from the hospital. And you probably hate that friend and her lazy baby. I want you to know that I was that friend. My friend Eileen and I had babies at the same time; mine was the sleeping and smiling sort, and hers was the car alarm on a Maserati. She did not sleep for the first six months of his life. Obviously the better mother, I liked to offer suggestions: "Have you tried rocking him?"

I also want you to know that life is fair and that my second child was hell-on-wheels colicky. And that he almost never screams now. I want to march him over to you in his full eleven-year-old glory and say, "Look!" I'd make him show you how he can dribble with both hands and how he can calculate the per-glass cost of a bottle of wine. (Have you ever tried to divide by 4 ½?) He has a strong sense of how to solve his own problems and a heroic pain tolerance. Skills learned during infancy? Maybe. I want you to know that he now wakes up on a Sunday morning, grabs a granola bar and lets me sleep until I'm good and ready to face the day.

Most importantly, I want you to know that if you have any money at all — money you've been saving for a vacation, retirement or a medical procedure — hire help. Indulge in the pure luxury of a nap. Don't sneak the nap. Instead, shower and put your pajamas on in the middle of the day. If money is not here to help us repurchase a bit of lost sanity, I don't know what it's for. And when you wake up, take that screamer back in your arms. He won't have forgotten you.

And I'm sorry for reading your mind, but I can see the question you really want answered. No, you will never have your life back the way it was before. Never. Nor will you want it back. Just hang in there.

LIFE ON THE GOD SQUAD

I think it's kind of funny that the same community that thinks seven-year-old kids need a snack in the middle of a sporting event also expects those same kids to top off a six-hour school day with 75 minutes of religious instruction. Imagine being in the second grade: word problems, spelling lists, alphabetical order! You're finally sprung at 3 p.m. and race onto the playground like a pack of uncrated puppies ... only to be marched over to church to hear the likes of me talk about God. Some days I feel almost as sorry for them as I do for myself.

I've taught CCD for nine years. When I tell people that, I feel like a different sort of a person, like maybe a person with a more conservative manner of dress, a clean house and a less colorful vocabulary. People generally think I'm kidding, and they wait for the punch line like I'm going to make C-C-D stand for something wacky. CCD (FYI) stands for Confraternity of Christian Doctrine, which I am sure of because I just Googled it. It's a weekly religion class that Catholic kids have to go to if they don't go to Catholic school.

This year I co-taught a class with my friend Emily. They gave us 15 children, 12 of whom are boys, presumably because she's a professional athlete and I'm paying off a staggering karmic debt. I know a few things about little boys, and one of them is that they cannot sit for very long. If at all. Asking little boys to sit and listen at 3:45 in the afternoon is like asking a coop full of chickens to perform Swan Lake. There are phrases that we repeat constantly: "Please sit back down. Please get off the desk. We can talk about who's lost the most teeth if there's time at the end of class." (The rate of tooth loss at this age is alarming.) "Yes, that clock on the wall is actually moving."

I'm not at all prone to self-sacrifice, so I wouldn't keep at it year after year if there wasn't some sort of a payoff. I like teaching CCD in that same way you might like camping. It seems like a shiny, wholesome idea at first. You over-prepare and purchase a bunch of supplies that you don't really know how to use. You slog your way up a mountain, trying to ignore the blister that is forming at the back of your wet sneaker. You want to give up, because really why in the world would you put yourself through such torture? In your darkest moments, you're worried that someone's going to get hurt. Teaching CCD is actually exactly like that. With 15 kids strapped to your back.

But then something happens, an unexpected view or a shooting star. Sometimes they'll surprise me by connecting a complicated concept like forgiveness to their own lives. Or they'll start to understand God as someone good, as a part of themselves and everything around them. I once had a student who noticed how the leaves come back on the trees to give us shade just in time for the hot summer. "God is thoughtful," she said. I caught my breath at that unexpected view.

The first class I ever taught is now finishing the tenth grade. I ran into one of the girls from that class on Mother's Day, and I had to get on my tippy toes to say hello to her. I remember her six-year-old face, terrified, on the very first day. I remember when she got a new puppy and brought him into class to show me. When she's 50, I'll look at her and remember that face and that puppy.

This year's merry band of maniacs just had their First Holy Communion. As the ceremony was starting, one of the boys gave me a hug before he'd had a chance to think better of it. Call it Stockholm Syndrome if you want, but I will remember that hug and every single tooth he lost this year when I see him dressed up again for the prom. The trek's been totally worth it.

College Admissions Mania

always wondered why parents went so mental when their kids were applying to college. I tended to give them a knowing smile, the "knowing" part being that I knew there was no way I was ever going to act like that. If I asked a question about where their kid was applying, they'd reply with a practiced, "We are not discussing it," like they were members of a covert ops team. As with all other stages of raising children, you just don't get it until you get there. I write this sitting next to a son who is perched on the edge of 11th grade, and I admit there's a good chance I'm going to go a bit mental myself.

I take solace in the fact that the same parents who go berserk during their kid's senior year are completely Zen a year later. They say things like, "Oh it all works out" and "There's a great school for every student." And I notice that their collective hair is starting to grow back where they'd previously been tearing it out. I just want to fast forward to that stage. I want to grab hold of that Zen and cloak myself in it for the duration of the next year.

Unfortunately, I have a history of going a bit overboard. Fact: when I was 16 and going through the college admissions process myself, I completely lost my mind. I applied to a dozen colleges and sucked up to every admissions officer that visited my school. While I'm being honest, let me just say that cookies may have changed hands. When decision time came, I camped out on the curb waiting for the mailman. The first envelope to arrive was a rejection. From my safety school.

Everything went silent.

And so began a period of time when I questioned my basic worth as a human being, the likelihood of my amounting to anything at all, and my right to breathe the air on this planet alongside the "accepted ones." It's disturbing now to think of how deeply I internalized this rejection. It was like I could verify my lack of value based on the politely worded language in that rejection letter.

Long story short, I got into another college and pinned my self-worth on their approval. Phew! That was close!

Recalling this dark time, why on earth would I think I wouldn't go nuts when my child goes through this process? The sane part of parents knows that our children are wonderful, complex beings, with value that is infinite and separate from the whims of college admissions officers. Our kids will thrive in any number of environments and grow up to be bigger, more knowledgeable versions of who they already are. The crazier side of us worries that this is somehow about us, that our child's admissions results will be a report card that either rewards us for driving to violin lessons or penalizes us for all those hours spent watching reruns of game shows.

One thing I hope to remember, besides the fact that this is not about me, is the fact that it's harder now. I don't know how it's possible that so many things can be easier when this thing is so much harder, but it is. The ugly truth about my generation is that few of us would be accepted to our alma matters today. I don't care if your first name's "Carnegie" and your last name's "Mellon," you'd probably be waitlisted now.

This adds to our stress because we know that our kids have to be twice as smart and accomplished as us we were. I do alumni interviews for my college, and these kids come at me with their state science award and their orchestra compositions and the import/export business they started while volunteering in Africa. I nod as if to say, "Yeah, I did that too." And by "that" I mean I went to the beach a lot.

I'm not quite engaged in the college thing yet. I'm looking at it from a reasonably safe distance, clutching the words of those Zen parents like the hand of a child who's about to run out into traffic. I write this as a reminder to myself and to my children that life is not pass/fail, and that it is so much more often circular than straight. And that the smartest person I know attended a college with a 73 percent acceptance rate.

My Super-Embarrassing Mom

Why is it that when you turn 12, your mom becomes so embarrassing? She asks too many questions, wears that blouse in front of your friends and waves goodbye in the loudest possible way. I feel the collective pain of the twelve-year-old community, because when I was that age my mom was so, so embarrassing.

For starters, she looked about ten years younger than all the other moms, with Farrah Fawcett's hair instead of Dorothy Hamill's. She was prone to tying that hair in pigtails, she disco danced and she listened to my music while driving carpool. She completely butchered the words to Dr. Hook while boogying her shoulders from side to side. You can imagine my distress.

While my friends swooned over the fact that I had the coolest mom ever, I secretly fantasized about what it would be like to have one of the other, more muted moms. With their mom haircuts and cardigan sweaters, these moms seemed to know their place. They'd fall in line at pick up in sensibly colored station wagons, sporting nothing more fashionable or eye catching than a little simulated wood paneling.

My mom would appear in the line up in her powder blue Chevrolet Monte Carlo, like a Skittle in a bowl of almonds. Even as a kid I was fascinated by this car choice. I mean, weren't station wagons standard issue? Not only was she driving a sedan, but it was a two door, the kind where the person in the passenger seat had to get out and fold forward the whole seat any time anyone wanted to get in or out. To this day, I don't think I know anyone with three kids and a two-door car. The Monte Carlo was fabulous and impractical, my mother personified.

Truth be told, there was never a day in my life that I did not fully appreciate the supreme awesomeness of my mom. These were my words at

12, and I have no better words today. She was beautiful and brilliant and funny and strong. From an early age, I saw her as a softer, hotter Statue of Liberty. She did plenty of mom things like cooking, sewing and listening — unfortunately, just not out on the playground where everyone could see.

You'll be glad to hear that since I've been a mom, I have not driven anything but a station wagon. You would never notice me in the traffic circle. I am more fashion neutral than fashion forward, and I've been rockin' the same pair of sensibly colored corduroys for years. Yet I have somehow managed to become infinitely more embarrassing than my mom in the most hideous possible ways.

My twelve-year-old self recoils at the sight of me. For starters, I've written two books that include kissing. It's actually not just kissing, but teenagers kissing. I am also incapable of keeping my mouth shut in the car. I've tried, but it's like the hinges of my jaw don't allow for it. Throw in a regular column in the local paper, a mad crush on a fictional vampire and a noisy presence on social media, and I'd say I've outdone my mom by a factor of ten.

So what compels us to such outrageous behavior? Can't the over-40 set just settle in and back off the scene? The truth is that 40-plus candles look a lot different now that the birthday cake is mine. I am the exact age that my mom was when I was 12, and I'm still just a kid. It's not that I'm out to mortify my kids; I'm just not as old as they think I am. Sure, I've been known to sing in the car to a couple of jazzy Top 40 tunes. But in my mind, it's still my music, not theirs. I mean Rihanna is closer to my age than she is to my kids', right? (No need to correct my math, but thanks for paying attention.)

It's been said that we are all destined to grow up to become our mothers. God I hope so. I think my mom understood that you just have to do what you want to do in life to be happy, and that you can't always play to your critics. And if those critics are 12, you're not going to win that battle anyway. Had she spent those years indoors, knitting in a nice beige cardigan, I would have been embarrassed by that too.

Motion to Limit the Use of the Word "Amazing"

B eing a contestant on a reality TV show is an amazing journey. I know this because, when interviewed, each and every one of those contestants (win or lose) says what an amazing journey it's been. I've never been on one of those shows, so I'm going to take their collective word for it.

When I was watching the election returns last week, I was shocked to find that the conceding candidates had also, in fact, just completed an amazing journey. They said it again and again, like they were standing next to Ryan Seacrest. The journey included the decision to run for office, the development of a platform and a lost election. Interesting? Sure. Amazing? No. There were only two ways the election could have gone. But again, I've never run for office.

Here's what I have done: I've been married with kids. So when I see my Facebook friends wishing their amazing husbands a happy anniversary, I take pause. When I see "Happy Birthday to the most amazing nine-year-old in the world," I think *what gives?* Is everybody's family amazing but mine? What, I wonder, is so amazing about these people?

Just to be clear: Amazing (adj.) Causing great surprise and wonder. Astonishing.

I picture these husbands swooshing into the bedroom in tights and capes. Maybe they clean the gutters dressed like Liberace while spinning plates in one hand. "Amazing" connotes a bit of flash. It suggests that an unforeseen "ta-da!" is just around the corner at all times. This kind of thing almost never happens in my house. My husband and children are good, even excellent, but I just can't remember the last time any of them pulled a rabbit out of a hat.

My husband is not a "ta-da!" kind of guy. His superpower is his ability to make the perfect joke in the most tense possible situation, thereby returning all participants to equilibrium. The value of this power cannot be overstated, and the first few times I experienced it, I have to admit I was amazed. But now it happens so regularly that there's probably another word for how I feel about it. After the eighth or ninth time Superman stops a train from running over your girlfriend, you are no longer amazed. Maybe it's "grateful" we're looking for?

Actually my favorite thing about my family is its unamazingness. They are consistent. The kid who says he'll be home at midnight, walks through the door at 12:15. I know what to expect. They wake up, get dressed, eat bacon and leave their stuff out in the rain in such a consistent matter that I'd be astonished if they didn't do these things.

After all these years, if my husband was constantly amazing me, I think it would kind of get on my nerves. "Look, honey, I painted a reproduction of the Mona Lisa on our front door!" "Check me out, I'm entering the house through the chimney today!" *That's amazing, honey. Now stop it!*

Same goes for that amazing children's movie you just saw. I understand that it was good, and that you liked the music and the little talking animal.

But were you really amazed that it all worked out in a happily ever after fashion? Were you amazed the princess didn't end up living alone, hoarding mayonnaise jars and caring for cats? Really?

It's clear why I don't wish my husband happy anniversary on Facebook, apart from the fact that he'd never see it. We've gotten to a place where it's hard to talk without hyperbole, because the truth seems a little dull. *Happy anniversary to my consistently good husband!* That would be the truth. *Thanks for entering the house through the front door like you're supposed to.* What would people think?

I'll tell you who's amazing: The Amazing Spider-Man. It's in his name. He can shoot webs out of his wrists and use them to get around. He can be glum and sort of untalkative, but still keep Mary Jane's interest. I've seen him kiss upside down! That guy, and only that guy, is amazing.

THE INSTRUCTION BOOKLET

Nothing makes me feel like I need to get out of the house more than trying to get out of the house. All a sitter really needs is a map and a photocopy of my calendar so she knows who needs to be where, when. So why do I feel compelled to compile a small instruction booklet every time I leave someone new in charge. It sounds crazy, but a mom's job is much more complicated than it appears.

Mothering is not brain surgery — there are actually schools that you can go to that will teach you how to perform brain surgery. For mothering, all we've got is the school of hard knocks. You can apprentice for the job if you have younger siblings, babysit or watch TV, but most of it you have to learn the hard way. It's a sticky, three-dimensional art project, not a science. After years of on-the-job training, I have a lot figured out. And it has very little to do with what's on my calendar.

You start small in this job, usually with just one child who eats and sleeps. After a few months, you get brave enough to throw in Gymboree on Thursday mornings at 9:30. It's a big deal. My husband used to say with a mix of pity and envy in his voice, "So what have you two got going on for this week?" I'd reply, as if I was Secretary of State, "Well, you know we have Gymboree on Thursday. 9:30." What I didn't tell him is that I was secretly concerned about getting there at all, what with naps, the unpredictable weather and such.

Then you have another baby, and you honestly don't know how you'll ever get out of the house, get them both bathed, make dinner. But slowly you learn. You get stronger — savvy even — as you gain confidence that maybe you can do this. You know better than to rely on one pacifier. You move your jewelry to someplace where they won't be likely to grab it, lick it and toss it in the trash. And, as you learn, your brain starts to loosen up. You let go of your expectations of perfection and make room for lots of other information. Thursday is no longer Gymboree day. Thursday is: recycling (remind Kid One), basketball for Kid Two, library day for Kid Three and your last chance to feed anyone protein before the Friday pizza bender.

My tome to the sitter includes the calendar, of course, but has tons of additional information, because I can't send her in cold: When you leave for school, take the baseball stuff with you because if you go back home to get it, everyone will take their shoes off, and you'll never get them back in the car. Speaking of shoes, Kid Three has a tendency to take his shoes off in the car and tuck them out of sight under the driver's seat. So, before you make yourself crazy (and late) looking under couches for his shoes, look in the car. Kid Two will text you right as you are coming to pick him up from school to ask if he can go to Jack's house. So don't rush to pickup, it's a waste of time. No matter how lucid Kid One seems when you wake him up in the morning, he's going to fall back asleep the second you leave his room. Check back ten minutes later.

It takes time to season a mom. A seasoned mom doesn't react strongly to dirty hands or lost socks anymore. She has her radar up for big stuff and stays in touch with the even more seasoned moms so she can brace for what's coming. She avoids conversations that involve gossip about children, because she's had a few knocks on her own door. She's got a lot in her head and knows in her heart what pitfalls may be ahead for each child. She knows because she's been at this awhile.

Just as I'm pulling out of the driveway, I get an email about a birthday party I'd forgotten and (what?!) noon dismissal. I text the sitter an amendment to the aforementioned document. I'm on the highway by the time that I realize I forgot to tell her about the shoes being hidden under the driver's seat. Oh well, she'll figure it out.

The College Essay

As the parent of a rising high school senior, I've been to my fair share of college information sessions. The admissions officer always concludes with the same set of comments about the application: namely, that the college essay must capture your true and authentic voice and reveal the essence of who you really are. Exactly that line, 100 percent of the time.

I look over at my son, his eyes glazed over. I love this kid, and the essence of who he really is astounds me. But there is no way in hell that he, flipping through his Instagrams and quietly plotting his next meal, is going to have an easy time summing up his essential him-ness in 500 words.

Heck, I'm middle aged and I am just beginning to find my voice. Show me a seventeen-year-old kid who's able access his true and authentic voice in a way that shares the essence of who he really is, and I'll show you a kid who maybe doesn't need to go to college.

My college essay went something like this:

I am the student body president of my high school. In this capacity it has been my job, along with the rest of the student council, to review our school's honor code. Upon this review, we found that a discrepancy existed between the school's policies on cheating and stealing. Heretofore, this had not been addressed. I strive to excel in all areas of my life, and I hope to bring this energy to college so that I can make an impact there as well.

They read this, and they let me into college. "Every class could use a good narc," they must have said.

If I had really wanted to share my seventeen-year-old essence in my true authentic voice, I would have submitted this:

I'm so tired from all this schoolwork and this thing with the student council. I'm sorry I even brought it up, because now the whole honor code needs to be rewritten. Luckily Michele Jaffe is senior class president and smarter than me, and she'll do it. Whatever, Michele. My friends and I go to the beach a lot. My friend Julie and I like to stop for grilled cheese and fries on our way, and we've found that one place has better grilled cheese and another has better fries, so we stop twice. I think it's important to know what you want and go out of your way to get it. There's a boy I like, and I really hope he calls me. Also, I'd like to go to college because it's time to move out and my friends are all going.

This is the girl that showed up on campus, the one with the two-part plan for procuring the best in fried food. There was more to me at this point, most of which I can only see in retrospect. There were buds of character traits, hints of interests. But, at 17, they were not clear to me in a way that I could have explained to a team of admissions officers thousands of miles away.

I think a better way to get to know these kids would be to ask a series of questions about their habits. "How often do you make your bed?" would be a good place to start. Studies show that people who make their beds have a whole host of positive life habits. And it might shed a little light on the kids who describe themselves as "dedicated to service." If you really wake up in the morning looking for new ways to serve, you probably start by making your bed. Zero percent of the teenagers currently living in my house makes their bed on a regular basis.

So my kid is going to write this essay in the next few months. I've been politely asked not to help, which makes me want to strangle him and hug him at the same time. I hope he gets across some of the real things about himself. He likes math, but not as much as he likes his friends. He likes history, but not as much as he likes Chipotle. That's the kid who's going to show up at college, ready to figure the rest out.

Help! They're Listening!

I don't mean to brag, but my kids totally listen to me. It would be nice if this communication happened while we were sitting together by the fire, with me sharing decades of hard-earned wisdom, and them taking it in with smiles of appreciation. But no, they listen, but never at the right time.

I used to suspect that there was a barrier, a semipermeable membrane that separated my children's ears from the stuff I say. Reminders of tasks, any variety of nags and warnings of impending injuries didn't seem to form the right shapes to pass through. Conversely, the sound of an ice cream truck six miles away, or the first three notes of the Spongebob Squarepants theme song were perfectly shaped to slide right in and elicit an immediate reaction.

Now I wonder if it's even simpler than that. Like soccer simple. I wonder if the friendly advice and folksy life lessons that I deliver directly to their ears are diverted by a small but nimble goalie. Direct shots are easily caught. The only things that my kids hear come indirectly, like a ball shot high in the corner off of someone else's head.

I take a lot of direct shots. I tell them to put their laundry away, that I'll be ten minutes late to pick them up from school and that swinging a golf club in the house is a bad idea. I'll stand right in front of them and say, "I'm going to the market." They will reply as if they've heard, but ten minutes later I'll get a text in the produce aisle: "Where are you?"

I tell them to be kind. I tell them not to judge people, that it's not our job to decide how other people should live their lives. I tell them to see the good in people, no matter what. They stare blankly at my enlightenment.

But recently, when I was leaving the house to go celebrate an acquaintance's birthday, one asked, "You're going to meet her? Isn't she the one you think is kind of passive aggressive?" Another added, "… and braggy, since she bought that summer house …" How did those words get to their ears? Those comments that were made in whispered tones to someone else made it past the goalie. Score one for pettiness.

It seems that my children hear and take in literally every word that I don't direct at them. As they have multiplied and grown, I've realized that I'm never completely out of earshot, and they are never as completely engrossed in their TV show or schoolwork as I think. The words I choose, like the way I react to a setback or respond to a compliment, are all being recorded behind those seemingly tuned-out eyes. It can make you feel a little paranoid.

I should have cleaned up my act when my oldest son was two years old. One night he finished his spaghetti dinner and asked for more. I obliged, and he stared in awe at the second large plate of spaghetti sitting in front of him. He exclaimed, "Holy shit! That's a lot of noodles!"

I was horrified. Who could he have been around that would use that kind of language? How is it possible that this small genius not only absorbed this strange idiom but also used it perfectly in the face of all those noodles? He must have heard it more than once. I watched him dig into his noodles and thought, "Holy shit! He's listening!"

I will occasionally use this phenomenon to my advantage. I will stand at a misleadingly safe distance and tell my sister on the phone all about a new study that definitively links drug use to brain damage. I then carelessly leave the article near them, without actually handing it to them. It might get read.

They really do need to put their laundry away. It's piling up, and I've delivered this message in every direct way I know how. Here's hoping this crosses their path.

After Graduation, the Leaving Period

A year ago, a friend of mine whose child had just graduated from high school suggested I write an article about this big milestone. I thought about it and decided to wait. It would have been like writing a guidebook about Paris based on internet research, without actually going there and seeing the light, smelling the bread. A year later, my son has just graduated from high school. Let's just say I've seen the light. I assume that's why there are tears in my eyes all the time.

Okay, not all the time. Because this moment is actually a dream come true. Since the first day I was nauseated from prenatal vitamins, I've dreamed of seeing him grow up, finish high school and then move out into the world to finish becoming who he is. I've used up every birthday candle, every dandelion and every stray eyelash on this particular wish. He turned out to be a person beyond my imagination with his own talents and quirks and wonderful friends. He set a goal, he never slept, and here we are, victorious at the finish line. Ugh, it's the worst.

I've seldom had such mixed feelings, and such is the mind of a parent in the middle of the leaving period. This leaving period is characterized by equal parts joy and grief. A month of celebrations will culminate in the dreaded trip to Bed Bath and Beyond. That trip carries with it so much meaning that it's almost like a sacrament. *You have prepared yourself for this moment, my child, let us wander the aisles and purchase extra long sheets for your journey.*

The leaving period is a little like the very, very end of pregnancy. We'd wished for that pregnancy, tried for it, celebrated it. We measured our progress and couldn't wait for the moment that we get to see it to fruition. But in the last few minutes before delivery, we might have a feeling that maybe this wasn't such a good idea. It occurs to us that this is going to be really painful. And it's too late, there's no place for that baby to go but out.

Because the thing is, he's too big to stay here. He is almost 18 years old and about five inches taller than anyone else in the house. I might go so far as to say that he's outgrown us. He is still our child, but he is no longer a child in our house. He makes his own plans, he's on his own schedule. He's a separate ball of energy who barrels through the door, makes us all laugh and takes his brothers out for ice cream. He's no longer part of the routine; he feels like a treat.

And he's been leaving for a long time. High school begins a slow retreat, like the water draining from a tub. You barely notice as it's happening, and then suddenly you shiver and feel a little raw. Once they're in high school, they wake up, race out the door and come home to eat. By the time you're clearing the table, someone says, "Wait, where'd he go?" For a while now, my son has sounded like the car peeling out of the driveway.

So it actually feels right that he's going. Awful and terrible and the worst thing I've ever done without an epidural, but right. My takeaway from sitting in the middle of this leaving period is that it's okay to feel two ways. It's the way you feel when you sell the home you loved so that you could go off on a new adventure. In any transition, there's a period of holding onto the hand of the thing you are supposed to be letting go.

My husband has been saying for years that he's going to pull a Rodney Dangerfield and go "Back to School" when our son leaves. We all laugh because we like to pretend he's kidding. The truth is we can't tag along. We won't be those parents who call his professors. We won't be those parents who show up some weekend, unannounced. I know this because we've been asked nicely.

Growing up in a Marriage

When I was 25, newly engaged and registering for wedding gifts, I chose two sets of champagne glasses — fancy crystal ones and the cheaper, boxed ones for every day.

Yes, you read that right. In my mind, we'd definitely need everyday champagne glasses, like for Mondays.

Marriage isn't exactly what I thought it was going to be 20 years ago when I stood up in front of all those people and promised to be married forever. Marriage was an idea attached to a big party. My boyfriend and all my friends would be there to see me in a really big dress. Turns out "married" and "forever" were concepts I hadn't grown into.

Romantic relationships progress like life, starting in infancy and finally reaching maturity. When I met Tom, I attached to him the way a toddler might attach to a strategically placed candy bar in the supermarket checkout aisle. You couldn't have pried him out of my hands if you'd tried. I was afflicted by that mad, crazy infatuation that is probably the friendly cousin of the flu.

Like a little kid with no sense of object permanence, I could barely stand it if he left the room. I decided to marry him after about a week, but kept that to myself as best I could. We were engaged in nine months, married nine months later. I couldn't understand why the whole thing took so long.

This engagement and newlywed period brought our relationship into adolescence. It's that time when you're pretty sure you know what life's going to look like, mainly because you watched a lot of "Dynasty" as a kid. As I recall, this period was characterized by a lot of getting: getting jobs, getting engaged, getting presents, getting to go on a honeymoon. We fought about who forgot to fill up the ice tray and solved the problem by moving into an apartment with an icemaker. Why couldn't everyone be as good at being married as we were?

Then life happens. There are beautiful things like children and long walks and a canon of inside jokes that don't get old. But also banks fail and people get sick. Maybe one of you forgets to renew the other's commuter parking permit. Whatever forces a relationship into adulthood is usually this other, darker side of the marriage vows, the ones we kind of mumbled through because they'd never apply to us. We'd be richer, not poorer, obviously. We had two sets of champagne glasses after all.

When life starts to happen, you learn a lot about who your partner is. It's no longer Saturday night all the time. Adulthood can feel like a string of Mondays. Once you've moved through a patch of real life with someone, you learn a lot about the depth of their kindness, the strength of their integrity and the staying power of their sense of humor. It's in this moment that you stop sweating stuff like the ice trays.

You may not have seen these qualities in the infancy of a relationship, as you were blinded by id and roses and that thing that feels like the flu. 21 years ago, it never occurred to me to wonder if my new boyfriend would someday help take care of my disabled brother. Or how he'd react when my mom died. Or if he'd mind my sharing every thought I have about our family on the internet, should the internet turn out to be a real thing.

With so much good stuff invested over these 20 years, I've let go of the nonsensical way he manages the recycling. He's let go of the whimsical way I put away groceries. Couples who can get through the commuter parking permit thing are above such pettiness. We don't worry about whether we have things in common. I don't golf, and he doesn't read, but we have the same address, the same kids, the same plumber who never shows up. At this point, we pretty much have the same life story.

Marriage, as it turns out, is more than just a really long, legally binding date. We are a going concern, each other's next of kin. Next week we'll celebrate our 20th anniversary. It's on a Wednesday, so thank goodness for those everyday champagne glasses.

The Hazards of the Bumper Sticker

The other night, I was driving up to my house and saw a man unloading garbage from his car into the dumpster at the construction site next door. Is this a crime? Probably. Am I the Sheriff? No. He turned his head away from my headlights so that I couldn't ID him in a lineup, just in case. What he didn't know is that, at 15 miles per hour, I had a chance to read his entire biography on the back of his car.

The only reason I slowed down to look is that I have an unusual interest in bumper stickers. You could almost call it a hobby. I have a collection of about 50 great ones, all which I find hilarious and none of which are on my car. I'm generally fascinated about how much information people post about themselves on their rear windows. They are mostly for fun (Life is Good!), or for bragging (insert fabulous vacation destination here), but if you're going to be on the wrong side of the law, you should really be careful. I don't have access to technology that would let me run his plates, Cagney and Lacey style, but here's the data I gathered in 12 seconds:

His oval "RYE" sticker identifies him as one of approximately 7,500 males that currently live in Rye, New York. Another sticker told me where his kids go to school, narrowing my search down to 300 dads. The soccer ball on the gas cap eliminated no one, but the sticker advertising specifically which travel soccer team his child played for narrowed the choices down to 12 dads. Now I'm not that interested, but I'm pretty sure that with one phone call, I could figure out which of those 12 dads drives a minivan and is affiliated with that impressive southern university. Gotcha!

The only way he could have made this easier on me is if he had the stick figure family bumper sticker. That thing might as well include your blood type and your Social Security number. I've spent a lot of time in traffic marveling at the choices that the driver in front of me has made to identify her family. I've even been on the stick figure website to look through the choices, so I know what she's been through. They replicate your family in a very specific line drawing that you've compiled from 3,000 variations. I'm not sure that genetics even gives us that many possible options.

I start by choosing the size and shape of my body and the exact cut of my hair. They want to know if I have straight hair or straight hair with layers. The distinction eludes me, so I go on to choose a personal interest for each of us. At this point in the ordering process, I imagine most people just log out. I mean this is a bumper sticker, and here I am asking myself existential questions about who I really am. I have a lot of interests. Am I supposed to pigeonhole myself with one and then paste it onto my car? I am more complex than that triangular lady with the shopping bag! I like cooking, but not for children; I like the Wall Street Journal, but only on Saturday; I like sports, but only as a spectator and only if it's not too cold or wet outside. I like bumper stickers, reality TV and ironing. There are no icons for that person. I'm at once annoyed and delighted that I'm not among the choices for "adult female" on this website.

As I start to design my husband, I'm generous with the amount of hair I place on his head. I can make him a golfer, a guy with a lawnmower or a businessman, but none of those get to his essence. His likeness would include all of those things, while holding a clicker and a martini glass. And he's only got two hands. I give up at this point, wondering again why I would want the person in the car behind me to know how my husband spends his time.

Bottom line: if you have a tendency to do anything that could be described as surreptitious, you should probably keep identifying markers off your car. Last spring there were a couple of teenagers who liked to park in front of my house for a smoke before school. They drove a very popular car, but it had two distinct bumper stickers on the back. If I were so inclined, I could have identified them faster than you can say, "Cheech and Chong didn't finish high school."

I only have one bumper sticker on my car: "Peace is Possible." I've chosen this one because I think peace actually is possible and because I believe the message limits the amount of honking and gesturing on the part of the driver behind me when I've forgotten to yield at the traffic circle. And if someone ever spotted me on the wrong side of the law, the witness would have nothing to go on. "I didn't get her plates, Officer, but she seems to have an optimistic outlook about the future of mankind." They'll never find me.

Acknowledgements

This book was written in tiny pieces over a period of five years, beginning in The Rye Record. My most heartfelt thanks to Robin and Peter Jovanovich for hiring me to write for them. Besides mothering, it is the worst paying and most rewarding job I've ever had.

Thank you the shockingly talented Jill DiMassimo for her collaboration and for creating photographs for these essays. It has been fascinating to look at things through a true artist's eyes.

Thank you to Lee Woodruff for writing the foreword for this book. Writers that dive into and support other writers' work are the most generous possible human souls. Among those souls, Lee is the queen.

Thank you to my friend Taegan Goddard who is the person to whom I solemnly bring all of my big decisions. Thank you to Elizabeth Wellington for her eagle eye and her absolutely natural mastery of all things to do with the written word. And thank you to Valerie Henderson, avid essay reader and dear friend, for reading every single page.

Annabel Monaghan

Of course, thank you to the people who are scattered all over these pages: my children Dain, Tommy and Quinn, who ooze inspiration and humor. I hope you will accept these essays in lieu of scrapbooks. Seriously, those things are never getting done. To Tom, a lifetime of thanks for being the most beautiful part of this circus.

I suspect it's unusual to thank those who are now unloading the big dishwasher in the sky, but I would like to acknowledge my mom, Joany Lane. Her spirit, her love and her lifelong pursuit of fun are in every word I write.

About the Author

Annabel Monaghan writes for TheWeek.com, The Huffington Post and The Rye Record. She is the author of two novels for young adults, *A Girl Named Digit* and *Double Digit*, and she is the co-author of *Click! The Girls Guide to Knowing What You Want and Making it Happen*. Annabel teaches novel writing at The Writing Institute at Sarah Lawrence College and lives in Rye, New York with her husband and three sons.

...

Photography by Jill DiMassimo

www.jilldimassimo.shootproof.com

@jill_dimassimo

71926667R00114